BEFORE YOU SAY A WORD

Also by Erik Palmer

Researching in a Digital World

Teaching the Core Skills of Listening and Speaking

ERIK PALMER

BEFORE YOU SAY A WORD

A School Leader's Guide to Clear and Compelling Communication

Arlington, Virginia USA

2800 Shirlington Road, Suite 1001 • Arlington, VA 22206 USA
Phone: 800-933-2723 or 703-578-9600 • Fax: 703-575-5400
Website: www.ascd.org • Email: member@ascd.org
Author guidelines: www.ascd.org/write

Richard Culatta, *Chief Executive Officer;* Anthony Rebora, *Chief Content Officer;* Genny Ostertag, *Managing Director, Book Acquisitions & Editing;* Bill Varner, *Senior Acquisitions Editor;* Mary Beth Nielsen, *Director, Book Editing;* Katie Martin, *Editor;* Thomas Lytle, *Creative Director;* Donald Ely, *Art Director;* Georgia Park, *Senior Graphic Designer;* Circle Graphics, *Typesetter;* Kelly Marshall, *Production Manager;* Shajuan Martin, *E-Publishing Specialist;* Christopher Logan, *Senior Production Specialist;* Kathryn Oliver, *Creative Project Manager*

Copyright © 2024 ASCD. All rights reserved. It is illegal to reproduce copies of this work in print or electronic format (including reproductions displayed on a secure intranet or stored in a retrieval system or other electronic storage device from which copies can be made or displayed) without the prior written permission of the publisher. By purchasing only authorized electronic or print editions and not participating in or encouraging piracy of copyrighted materials, you support the rights of authors and publishers. Readers who wish to reproduce or republish excerpts of this work in print or electronic format may do so for a small fee by contacting the Copyright Clearance Center (CCC), 222 Rosewood Dr., Danvers, MA 01923, USA (phone: 978-750-8400; fax: 978-646-8600; web: www.copyright.com). To inquire about site licensing options or any other reuse, contact ASCD Permissions at www.ascd.org/permissions or permissions@ascd.org. For a list of vendors authorized to license ASCD ebooks to institutions, see www.ascd.org/epubs. Send translation inquiries to translations@ascd.org.

ASCD® is a registered trademark of the Association for Supervision and Curriculum Development. All other trademarks contained in this book are the property of, and reserved by, their respective owners, and are used for editorial and informational purposes only. No such use should be construed to imply sponsorship or endorsement of the book by the respective owners.

All web links in this book are correct as of the publication date below but may have become inactive or otherwise modified since that time. If you notice a deactivated or changed link, please email books@ascd.org with the words "Link Update" in the subject line. In your message, please specify the web link, the book title, and the page number on which the link appears.

PAPERBACK ISBN: 978-1-4166-3293-1   ASCD product #124026   n6/24
PDF EBOOK ISBN: 978-1-4166-3294-8; see Books in Print for other formats.

Quantity discounts are available: email programteam@ascd.org or call 800-933-2723, ext. 5773, or 703-575-5773. For desk copies, go to www.ascd.org/deskcopy.

Library of Congress Cataloging-in-Publication Data

Names: Palmer, Erik, 1953- author.
Title: Before you say a word : a school leader's guide to clear and compelling communication / Erik Palmer.
Description: Arlington, Virginia USA : ASCD, [2024] | Includes bibliographical references and index.
Identifiers: LCCN 2024007968 (print) | LCCN 2024007969 (ebook) |
 ISBN 9781416632931 (paperback) | ISBN 9781416632948 (pdf)
Subjects: LCSH: Oral communication—Study and teaching—United States. |
 School administrators—In-service training—United States. | Language arts—United States. |
 Public speaking.
Classification: LCC LB1572 .P348 2024 (print) | LCC LB1572 (ebook) |
 DDC 808.5/102437—dc23/eng/20240227
LC record available at https://lccn.loc.gov/2024007968
LC ebook record available at https://lccn.loc.gov/2024007969

---

33 32 31 30 29 28 27 26 25 24   1 2 3 4 5 6 7 8 9 10 11 12

Before You Say a Word

Preface vii

Part I: Planning the Message 1

   1. Who You Will Be Talking To 3

   2. What You Should Say 24

   3. What You Shouldn't Say 53

   4. How to Present Your Message 66

Part II: Delivering the Message 103

   5. The Vocal Skills You Need for Impressive Delivery 107

   6. The Nonverbal Aspects of Impressive Delivery 124

Afterwords 138

Acknowledgments 147

References 149

Index 151

About the Author 155

Preface

"Hey, don't blame the messenger!"

You've heard this phrase before. It's what people say when there's bad news to deliver—bad news that listeners don't want to hear.

In the school where I first worked, our team leader said it often. We chose Tom to be the representative for our combined 5th and 6th grade team, and he attended meetings with the other grade-level leaders and the principal. Often, he came back with reports of some new things we had to do—initiatives we had to implement, schedule changes to accommodate assemblies, and additional work required of us. For example, Tom once returned from a meeting and told us that we had to pick up morning playground duty.

"Parents are dropping their kids off well before school starts, and the playground is full. There is no supervision, and so if something happens, there is no one out there to help. Each grade level has to have one teacher out on the playground before school."

We got agitated and began to complain.

"That's outside our contract hours!"

"We have to prepare for the day."

"That cuts into planning time."

"Well then, tell the parents they can't drop their kids off early!"

This went on for quite a while. Seeing how worked up we were getting, Tom said, "Hey, don't blame me. I'm just the messenger." He used that phrase frequently. When someone argued that a schedule change would mess up their unit testing plans? "Hey, don't blame me. I'm just the messenger." When we learned the new reading assessment would be given the morning after Halloween trick-or-treating? "Hey, don't blame me. I'm just the messenger."

At the time, it seemed like Tom was right. Why vent at him when it was the new thing or directive that we hated? The new thing wasn't *Tom's* idea, and he had no power to change it. It was the *message* that was to blame, not Tom. Don't blame the messenger.

After a few years in education, I began to think differently. By then, I had received a lot of messages, many of which were undercut and sometimes ruined by the messenger. I saw good initiatives dead on arrival because of how poorly they were presented. I witnessed well-meaning administrators create ill will because of the way they spoke to the staff. I attended dreadful professional development sessions where people walked away with little because the presenters were so dull. I noticed that few paid attention during staff meetings because little seemed worth paying attention to.

Why This Book

During the COVID-19 pandemic, when meetings and presentations went online, it was more apparent than ever that weak speaking was a problem. Recall the disjointed Zoom meetings, webinars that seemed painfully long, the professional development videos that were boring and hard to watch. The poor-to-mediocre oral communication that was tiresome in person was even worse on the small screens of digital devices. So staff members, webinar attendees, and video watchers checked out, turned off their cameras and microphones, and moved on to amusing cat videos and online shoe shopping. Although school and district leaders had the communication tools necessary to move messages online, they lacked the foundational communication skills they needed to use those tools well. They didn't know how to be clear, engaging, and impressive speakers. I don't blame the tools. I blame the messengers.

Of course, I don't really *blame them* blame them. I believe these messengers—primarily teacher leaders and administrators—did the best they could. Steven Weber is an assistant principal at Rogers Heritage High School in Arkansas and a former assistant superintendent. Steven told me that "it is very challenging making the shift from teaching students to leading professional development and speaking with adults. Many educators are very nervous when they have their first few public presentations." Why? Because education leaders seldom get the training they need to do the job they have been given. Let me ask you: when, on your path to your leadership role, did you get specific help with oral communication skills?

Poor communication is a problem in many workplaces. In a survey reported in *Forbes* (Hoory, 2023), nearly 50 percent of respondents reported that ineffective communication decreased their job satisfaction; 42 percent said it affected their stress levels. Pause a minute and reflect. How many personal examples of poor on-the-job communication can you come up with right now? Can you think of staff developers who were ineffective? A particular workshop that bombed? Principals whose choice of words regularly antagonized or angered the staff? A presenter with a bizarre tic that you remember to this day? Teachers on the team who just rubbed each other the wrong way because of their communication style? What am I missing? I bet you have many examples of situations where the listeners just didn't get it . . . and it was the messenger who deserved the blame. I'm not suggesting that improved oral communication will solve all the problems in your building or district, but I am suggesting that we can do a lot to eliminate the poor verbal exchanges that get in the way of solving those problems.

Great speaking will not change your school culture, and this book doesn't make that argument. Actions do speak louder than words, and lip service to noble goals will never suffice. Nor is my purpose to give you slick speaking skills you can use to pull the wool over others' eyes. I only want to make sure that weak oral communication skills do not get in your way. I want you to be confident that you have presented the message you intend as powerfully and as well as possible. If the idea is rejected, it should be rejected on its merits rather than because of its presentation.

About This Book

Although most people don't think much about this, all speaking involves two distinct parts: one, preparing something to say and two, saying it. While this may seem obvious once I point it out, few people understand how profound that realization is. I can certainly think of times when I thought, "Wow, *that* was the wrong thing to say," as well as times when I thought, "That didn't come out the way I wanted it to." The first comment makes clear that I should have thought more *before* I opened my mouth. The second makes clear that the out-loud part went wrong. I can also think of times when I thought, "That was the ugliest PowerPoint I have ever seen," and times when I thought, "That speaker was impossible to listen to." Again, the first comment refers to something created *before* the talk while the second refers to how the speaker spoke. The first part of this book addresses the *before speaking* issues; the second addresses what to do *as you are speaking* to ensure a better reception.

This is a practical, experience-based book. I cite research, but I build my case on what education leaders have shared with me. You will hear from a central office leader, principals, education consultants, teachers on special assignment, instructional coaches, staff developers, and a lead counselor. These are people who have been there and faced the challenges associated with communicating with wildly diverse audiences. Together, we'll learn from their mistakes and from their successes. Every now and then, I'll insert a case study for you to ponder, and at the end of all chapters but this one, you will find a set of application exercises; some focus on the case studies, and others prompt you to connect what you've just read to your own practice.

If you have picked up this book thinking it might be for you, trust that it is. Yes, it will help you if you're an official school leader tasked with giving "leadership" talks before big audiences. Improved oral communication skills will help you when you are welcoming new students and parents at school orientation, facilitating a PLC, training teachers on how to give the state assessment, conversing in a breakout room at a conference, or sharing directives with your team, like my former colleague Tom. Strong speaking skills will also help you get more out of casual interactions with others in hallways, break rooms, and lunchrooms and turn them into opportunities for constructive communication that will positively affect school culture.

The fact is, being an effective messenger is important in nearly all education settings and all education roles. It's not important only for those in official leadership positions. Consider how the greeting delivered at a school's front desk can make or break a visiting parent's experience before a meeting or conference gets started. Remember that the counselor speaking briefly at Back to School Night may not have "leader" in her title, but as the face of the counseling department, she needs to be a competent and confident oral communicator. The concepts shared in this book will benefit these staff members and many others.

Additionally, I think the ideas here have a broad application beyond education. After all, how much of your day outside school involves speaking? Speaking is by far the number one language art and deserves much more attention than it gets. Yes, I want you to be able to craft and deliver powerful messages in the many different situations you face as a professional educator, but speaking well will benefit you wherever you are and whatever you are doing. You may need to give a toast at a bachelorette party, a eulogy at a funeral, a talk at a friend's retirement dinner, or a pep talk to your child. The suggestions here will apply to all of those situations as well.

And finally, as I wrote this book, I often thought, "But this point is obvious, isn't it? It's common sense." As you have no doubt discovered, common sense is often not common at all. If it is all so obvious, why would we see terrible oral communication failures all around us? Why would we hear the head of a prestigious grades 6–12 prep school say, in the opening minutes of her Day One welcome-back greeting, "Please remember to flush the toilet after you use it." (Message intended but not received: "I'm the right person to lead this school, and we are going to have a great year.") Why would a big-name author, speaking at a national conference and eschewing PowerPoint, repeatedly walk back to her computer to add another yet another point in illegible handwriting until the screen was entirely filled with scribbling that no one in the audience could read? (Message intended but not received: "These are great ways to improve school culture.") Why would a national organization create an instructional video in which a very dull speaker reads every word printed on every slide? (Message intended but not received: "This is a wonderful strategy that will help you in your work.") Why would a Zoom meeting speaker not notice that everyone had a close-up view of his desk, littered with fast-food trash? (Message intended but not received: Whatever he was talking about while the viewers were evaluating his eating habits.) In each of these instances, all of which I witnessed while I was writing this book, what was obvious to me was not obvious to the messenger. And in all of these communication failures, the messenger was to blame. So, let's get to work and learn how to be more effective messengers.

Part I

Planning the Message

In your role as a leader, coming up with a message topic is rarely a problem. Your purpose has been given to you: you must explain how the new state law affects the district, report the results of the state assessment, provide coaching on classroom management, and so on. Sure, sometimes there are options—*which funny stories do I want to tell at the Teacher of the Year Tea?*—but coming up with the topic is not usually the hard part of speaking. The bigger challenge is figuring out how to craft the message *well*. Does the opening command attention and create interest? Is all of the content meaningful and engaging? Are the words appropriate for the audience and occasion? Do the ideas flow logically? Does the closing leave a positive and lasting impression?

Because a well-crafted message has to do all these things, it's not surprising that few people are really good at impromptu speaking. It is difficult to create a talk on the spur of the moment, which is why an impromptu speech about an important matter can lead to a host of problems, ranging from misunderstanding to antagonism. We need time to come up with the right words to say. Even if we come up with the right words, ad-libbing may take us away from the intended message and open the door to foot-in-the-mouth moments.

A bumbling or boring or insensitive speech is a more serious problem for school leaders than it may seem. Consider that those you're speaking to may only hear your voice occasionally. Colleagues who have greater access to you might be able to say, "Once you get to know her, you'll see she knows her stuff," but the rest will use just a couple of talks to decide who you are and whether to trust your leadership. Those talks better be good.

Further, school leaders need to be especially careful creating messages for the high-stakes situations they and their colleagues face. One false step, one misstatement, can lead to irate parents, disillusioned staff, ineffective professional development, and other problems you've probably witnessed in your career.

However, you know better than I do that the job demands on school leaders do not allow them to spend a massive amount of time preparing every talk. Prioritization is key. Learn to recognize which talks require more careful construction. For example, it's likely you can devote less thought and time to preparing your seventh "Welcome, New Parents!" talk than to preparing a talk for a concurrent session at a national conference or preparing what you will say at a parent meeting about a divisive and potentially explosive topic. Better to invest time up front crafting the right message *before* you speak than to spend several times longer cleaning up a mess caused by bad communication.

This section offers some guidance about what school leaders must do before they ever say a word. I offer ideas to help you think differently about the kinds of messages you need to deliver in your leadership role, formal or informal. Following these suggestions will ensure that your message is solid and worth presenting, and it will give you confidence that your message will be understood *and* well received. We will focus on four questions:

- Who will you be talking to?
- What should you say?
- What shouldn't you say?
- How should you present the message?

These are simple questions that have complex answers. Carefully thinking about and answering them will ensure that your message will be worth delivering.

1

Who You Will Be Talking To

Most speakers begin by thinking, "I have something to say," and they focus on what they want to talk about. Powerful, effective speakers do things differently. They begin by thinking, "I need to understand my audience," and they focus on what the listening experience will be like for the people they'll be talking to.

Yes, many speaking occasions necessitate some required content. If you are leading a professional development session, for example, you will have information to convey or ideas to share. If you are leading a collaborative work group, you will have an objective to explain and pursue. Consider, though, that every time you convey information, share ideas, and explain and pursue objectives, you will do so within a particular context and before a particular audience.

You know what I mean about context. We have all been in situations where we decided *not* to mention a specific topic because we could sense our audience would not be receptive. For example, when my son told me he had just been rejected by the girl he wanted to take to the homecoming dance, I decided *not* to mention that he was supposed to have cleaned his room. His room was a mess, and I did have something to say about that, but the moment seemed wrong. You've likely seen your share of school leaders failing to recognize the wrongness of the moment for the message they had to communicate.

Here is an example from Gabrielle Price*, a counselor at a grades 6–12 private school in the Northeast United States. Gabrielle tells the story of a first-day-back in August when the schedule had all staff gathering for breakfast at 7:30 a.m. before beginning the day's official activities at 8:00 a.m. Most of the colleagues at the various breakfast tables hadn't seen each other all summer. Not surprisingly, many conversations spilled past the 8:00 a.m. start time, and staff members were still straggling in a few minutes past the hour. When the last teachers had settled, the head of school took the mic and opened with this: "Excuse me, but in this school, 'early' is on time, 'on time' is late, and 'late' is not tolerated." How do you think that message went over? What tone did it set? And do you think it was an effective way to communicate what the head intended to be an important community value?

An effective message is never created in a vacuum. The best ones require getting into the listeners' heads and designing messages with that specific audience in mind. Yes, this can be complicated, especially considering the varied audiences you need to address.

Steven Weber, the leader introduced in the Preface, cataloged all the situations in which he was expected to speak:

- At faculty meetings
- With curriculum planning teams
- With one student
- With the student body
- With parents/families
- Presenting to the board of education
- Delivering professional development
- At a retreat or during team-building activities
- One-to-one meetings with the superintendent

Steven also noted that not all of his speaking is done in person. In recent years, on-camera speaking via Zoom and YouTube videos has

---

*This is a pseudonym.

taken up a larger share of communication with district colleagues, students, and families. When I asked him to put together a list of all the occasions education leaders might have to speak during just the final month of a school year, his response underscored the astonishing amount and variety of speaking these positions demand:

- Announcing staff resignations and retirements
- Recognizing career and technical education (CTE) students and announcing each one's post-graduation school or work assignment
- Remarks at the Annual Retiree Banquet
- Making the Teacher of the Year Announcement at various schools throughout the district
- Greeting (and impressing) rising high school students and their families when incoming 9th graders attend their orientation session and sign up for new courses
- Recognizing seniors at band and choir concerts and sporting events
- Recording videos to be shown on Jumbotrons or video boards at sporting events
- Presenting at school board meetings
- Having hiring conversations
- Giving remarks and having conversations at community meet-and-greets
- Speaking at school fundraisers and PTO meetings
- Speaking at school assemblies
- Giving remarks at elementary school assemblies
- Having one-on-one, post-evaluation conversations with staff
- Announcing new programs or curriculum for the next school year
- Conducting focus groups to discuss and gather feedback on written and taught curriculum
- Leading end-of-year celebrations and community partner/sponsor recognitions
- Giving remarks at appreciation luncheons
- Talking with families about student behavior/conduct issues
- Communicating with the media (usually at the central office level)

- Creating video pieces for the school's official social media accounts
- Communicating with the district office and the state department of education
- Communicating with elected officials—local, state, federal
- Speaking as a member of state or national organizations or advocacy groups
- Conducting leadership workshops and professional development sessions
- Giving remarks at high school graduation

It's an impressive list—and a daunting one, when you consider how varied these audiences are. And these are just what we might call "big talks." How about all the little talks leaders engage in daily? Those quick conversations in the hallway, the teachers' lounge, or the cafeteria? It's partly because school leaders wear so many hats and have so many different kinds of messages to communicate that they need to be adept at analyzing each audience, each listener, and designing talks specifically for them.

Big Picture Considerations

I want to begin by highlighting two high-level issues.

Who will you invite to receive your message?

Sometimes the audience is a given: students and their parents at New Student Orientation Day, members at the monthly meeting of the parent-teacher community organization (PTCO), attendees at the middle school band conference, and so on. But often, the audience is selected—and education leaders sometimes deliver messages to people who don't need those messages. I'm thinking specifically of a talk given to the entire staff about *not* parking in the spots reserved for building guests, even though the only car that had ever been seen in those spaces was Greg's. Why require all teachers to attend all meetings when the content at some meetings applies only to a few?

There are two simple questions you can ask to zero in on the *real* right audience:

- Who *needs* to hear this message?
- Who *will benefit* from hearing the message?

Limit your audience to those people.

What "hidden audiences" might there be?

As we'll delve into in a moment, the speaking occasion and the top-level label you give an audience can tell you only so much about who your audience really is. For example, if you're preparing to give remarks at a school board meeting, is your audience the board members? Is it the board members *and* the meeting attendees in the room? Or is it the board members, meeting attendees in the room, and families and community members watching at home via a livestream or a video recording? Which of these various audience factions is the most important to reach? Should your message incorporate "ed speak" in order to speak more precisely and efficiently with board members, who are fluent in it? Or should you avoid ed speak in order to communicate more effectively with the public listening in?

Mindset and Expectations

Before digging deeper into a thorough audience analysis, there are some foundational guidelines to keep in mind.

Begin with respect

I want to share three stories.

Story 1. I worked under five principals in the 11 years I spent at one school. All came in with a mission and a personal agenda. None of them reached out to staff with questions like "What initiatives have you tried recently?" or "What would you like to see happen at this school?" or "How can I help you succeed?" None of these new principals acknowledged that we, the staff, had a past and our own ideas about what the school needed or needed to do differently.

Story 2. I attended a conference in California when smartphone apps were in their infancy. Today, most of us have an app for every letter of the alphabet, but that was not the case back then. One speaker, presumably someone who wanted to be thought of as more with-it than most, said, "Here are 10 apps all teachers must have right now!" There was no awareness that some of us in the audience taught 6-year-olds and some taught 16-year-olds; some taught math and some reading; some came from schools where 87 percent of students qualified for free or reduced price lunch; and some taught at schools where students didn't think twice about hiring a limo to take them to homecoming. It was taken for granted that our needs were uniform, and so were the apps that would help address those needs.

Story 3. In the beginning of my consulting career, I went to watch Karla, a veteran presenter, deliver a day-long workshop to a large group of educators. The 300 attendees had paid a considerable fee to the educational outfit she worked for, and after watching her for a while and being unimpressed, I decided to sneak a peek at the evaluations that the district required attendees to complete. They were unanimous in declaring the day to have been a very expensive waste of time. When I gingerly mentioned these ratings to Karla, she said, "I don't give a s*** what they think."

There's a common theme to these stories, and I suspect you've already identified it: a lack of respect for the audience. While the first two speakers were not as profane as Karla, they shared her basic sentiment: "Here is what I have to say, and it doesn't matter to me who you are, where you come from, what you do, or what you think. I am the leader here, and your job is to listen to me." That attitude is far too common, and it is responsible for a lot of ill will felt by the people being led.

Basic respect

Your audience is made of individuals, and as individuals, they matter. Before you say a word, make sure you are coming from a place of empathy, caring, and collaboration. Be deliberate about this because it may require effort. As Steven Weber points out, "Many school administrators are adept at solving problems, [but] they are not experts at listening and showing empathy for the other person's perspective." I didn't love every decision my five principals made, and yes, I liked some teammates better than others, but I never talked to any of them without understanding that each had a history, dreams, issues, ideas, and feelings.

Listeners sense disrespect, and once they do, the speaker is doomed. A version of the Golden Rule applies here: *say to others what you would like others to say to you.* If you were in your audience, what would you want to hear? Are you introducing a new initiative, for example? Then identify the existing program that will be going away to make room for it. Are you explaining how a new law might limit what your history department can teach about certain topics? Then explain what the administration will do to back up teachers if issues arise. Fill in the blank: "If I heard ___, I'd be thrilled." Then respect the listeners' wishes and put those in the forefront of your mind.

Respect for listeners' expertise

Everyone you talk to knows more about some things than you do. They may know more about living with an extended family in one apartment or how to engage a roomful of 8th graders or how to run a classroom science lab or any number of things.

Part of understanding your audience is finding those areas of expertise and clarifying that you credit them for their strengths. This involves recognizing your limits, too. I can give you excellent advice about how to teach all students to become more competent and confident speakers. But if you ask me for help dealing with the social and emotional problems of high school students who lost a year and a half of in-person learning during the pandemic, I would not say a word. I would instead send you back to Gabrielle Price, the long-tenured school counselor. Gabrielle was there before the pandemic, during the pandemic, and after the pandemic. She knows the mental health issues of students. Though you may be the highest-ranking person in the room, you may not be the one best equipped to speak.

Take a minute now to think about a time during your career when an administrator came in to tell you (or a colleague) how to do your (or their) job better. When I do, I recall Ben, one of the five principals I referred to earlier, telling a veteran teacher how she ought to teach 8th grade math. Before moving into administration, Ben had two years of experience teaching 4th grade; Linda, the teacher, had 20 years of experience teaching math to 8th graders who were enormously successful by most math measures.

Let's go ahead and consider what was happening here. Ben, fresh from a conference presentation on instructional methods, came into Linda's classroom and said, "This is a better way to teach math, and here's how you need to change your math instruction." What do you think went on in Linda's head? I can't guarantee that Linda taught math in the most perfect way and that no improvement was possible, but I can guarantee that Ben failing to lead with an acknowledgment of Linda's experience and expertise and failing to ask her for her impressions after telling her about the presentation he saw was a *big* mistake. Ben's intentions were great. Maybe he learned about a way to reach struggling kids or a way to help all students master some concepts more quickly. Unfortunately, because of his approach, it's very unlikely that Linda was receptive.

Anticipate resistance and points of confusion

There are times when you have no choice but to tell listeners something they don't want to hear. If you understand your audience, you will know before you begin what will be unpopular, and you will be able to both build in answers to the likely questions and lay out possible remediation.

Here's an example. When I was teaching 6th grade science, my building principal, Nola, announced that all future report cards would include a letter grade and proficiency scores from 1 to 4 (1 = unsatisfactory, 2 = partially proficient, 3 = proficient, 4 = advanced). I thought that was reasonable. I knew that sometimes a student worked hard and earned an *A* grade yet wasn't as adept at science as some other students. A combination of a letter grade and a proficiency score, like

"A, 3," seemed like it would generate a better, fuller picture of the student's learning status. But the principal was not finished. She went on to explain that teachers would be required to give multiple proficiency scores within each subject. As a science teacher, I was supposed to give a proficiency rating on Content Knowledge, Use of Scientific Method, Use of Lab Equipment, Lab Safety, and Using Scientific Language. In other words, for each of the 130 students I had during my four science rotations, instead of one grade, I had to give six, including the overall letter grade for the marking period. Yes, that would mean 780 grades each quarter instead of 130. Predict my response and the response of all the other teachers.

Our principal also explained that there was no alternative approach possible, no opting out. This was the new grading system adopted by the school board. Faced with a bunch of disgruntled teachers full of comments, Nola had no way to change the decision, which wasn't hers, but she did invite a parent in the community who had a coffee cart business to attend the meeting. We all got lattes paid for by the district—a gesture we appreciated. School leaders can't always make everything OK, but they can try to soften the blow. Our principal knew us and did what little she could to communicate her understanding and solidarity.

Many district-level decisions reveal a lack of foresight and carry unrealistic expectations, fueling an unfortunate "us versus them" dynamic between school-based staff and their leaders in the district office, and between those in staff positions and members of the leadership team. If no one at the school board meeting ever says, "Hang on a second. How will teachers respond to this?" that is a problem. If the response is "It doesn't matter what the teachers say. We want to do this," then that is a bigger problem. Yes, there are some "Teachers must do this because the law requires it" decisions—see state-mandated testing—but for most districts, thousands, if not millions, of dollars have been wasted trying to push something on teachers that a bit of foresight and audience analysis would have immediately flagged as doomed. I'll pause and let you think of all the failed initiatives you have witnessed that audience analysis could have prevented.

Case Study

Jeannie was the principal at the school where I first taught. The school was big enough to require two assemblies when we had special presentations. Grades K–3 attended the first assembly, and grades 4–6 attended the second. Here's a paraphrase of how Jeannie addressed the first assembly:

> *Hello, boys and girls. Today we have a special presentation for you. It's called Ballet Folklórico. Do you know what ballet is? It is a kind of dance. And Folklórico is a funny-sounding word, isn't it? It is a Mexican word, and the dancers today come from Mexico. Do you know where Mexico is? It's a country right below our country....*

Yes, there are a couple of cringeworthy things in there, but let me share with you how she introduced the assembly to the second group, including my 6th graders:

> *Hello, boys and girls. Today we have a special presentation for you. It's called Ballet Folklórico. Do you know what ballet is? It is a kind of dance. And Folklórico is a funny-sounding word, isn't it? It is a Mexican word, and the dancers today come from Mexico. Do you know where Mexico is? It's a country right below our country....*

Yes, the principal gave the very same introduction to the older students as she'd given to the young ones. My students reacted by rolling their eyes. One of them looked at me and asked, "Why is she treating us like babies?"

A Practical Approach to Audience Analysis

In a sense, using the word *audience* is misleading. It suggests there is a single entity out there rather than a collection of individuals, varying in composition according to the type and occasion of presentation (e.g., faculty meeting, English Department meeting, book study group, parent advisory committee) and varying further as individuals within those subsets. To analyze the audience, then, means to understand the individuals who comprise it and how they may receive your messages differently. As noted earlier, there are times when we can think generically—all teachers will balk at a 600-percent increase in grading—but understanding individual differences will increase your scope and effectiveness as a messenger. I never present to the audience; I present to the individuals in that audience. It is more than a semantic difference.

So how do you learn about those individuals, their interests, their motivators? Let me share some ideas.

Get advance input on perspectives and priorities

How often do you ask for input as you craft your messages? How often do you ask for input from those whom you know have views that differ from your own? It is difficult to communicate with people if you don't understand them, their perspectives, and their priorities.

Let's say you want someone to explain some new tech tools to your staff. Of course, the school tech expert volunteers to do that job, and you select her to be an instructional coach. The problem, ironically, is that your tech expert is . . . a tech *expert*. She finds everything technology-related easy and intuitive and has no trouble with new tools. People can be blinded by their expertise to the degree that they can't prepare a message that serves and resonates with those who are novices in the area or may even be totally unfamiliar with the subject matter. In this case, the tech coach should find the least-techy person in the building and talk to them to get a sense of the kind of thinking that exists outside the tech-wizard brain.

Explore contrasting perspectives. Marquetta was my principal when I was a middle school teacher. She and I had very different opinions about many issues, a fact we both were aware of. Let me share a story that took place during a time when wearing pajama pants was fashionable in our middle school. A couple of teachers did not like this at all and talked the principal into adding pajama pants to the list of clothing that violated the school dress code. As a result, behavior that had been fine from September through January suddenly became not fine in February.

Students reacted. One 8th grade girl organized a Pajama Pant Protest Day, and dozens of students showed up wearing now-forbidden pajama pants along with buttons that announced themselves as pro-pajama-pants-wearing. Marquetta thought this was an outrageous violation of the rules... but before she started handing out suspensions (her first inclination), she came to me and asked what I thought. Although I was quite excited about this peaceful protest that I could turn into a civics lesson, I urged calm. I suggested we let the protest organizer know that Marquetta respected the child's opinion, ask the child what she thought might be a fair solution to the rule breaking, and otherwise just wait for the pajama-pants fad to fade away on its own. The result? No suspensions, an agreement to allow pajama pants on Wednesdays, and an issue that disappeared when the weather improved and we had to start worrying about shorts being too short.

This was a one-time event, but the practice of seeking staff members' perspectives on various issues is solid. Who on your staff do you reach out to for opinions? Taking another step back, do you invite classified staff—custodians, cafeteria workers, bus drivers—to your discussions about student behavior? Do you ask your counselors how they think others could help them in providing emotional support for struggling students? Do you seek out those who never speak at faculty meetings to learn from them? Look for those who differ from you in job responsibilities, beliefs, and temperament, and include their takes in your thinking as you craft your message.

Learning about every audience member

Nola guessed that the entire faculty would dislike the new grading system. But let's use a faculty meeting as an example of how varied a faculty is. Yes, they are all teachers—and from that data point alone, it's fair to say they they are pressed for time, they understand education jargon, they are committed to helping students, they eat all kinds of food placed in the teachers' lounge, and they want to leave early on Friday. But even with these commonalities, how many are

- Male?
- Female?
- English language arts teachers?
- "Specials" or electives teachers?
- Science teachers?
- Teaching the youngest students at your school?
- Teaching the oldest students at your school?
- Extroverts?
- Introverts?
- Married?
- Master teachers?
- Coaches or club sponsors?
- Willing to try anything?
- Thoughtful rule followers?
- Mavericks?

How many have

- Been teaching less than three years?
- Been teaching more than 14 years?
- A good sense of humor?
- Great rapport with students?
- A tendency to complain about students or parents?
- Serious issues in their lives outside school (e.g., divorce, illness, caretaking for an elderly parent)?

- Come to teaching as a second career?
- Children?
- Pets?
- Hobbies they're passionate about?

You will think of other descriptors. Pay attention and you'll notice that every audience you address is varied and complicated, characterized by all kinds of variables and motived by a whole range of factors.

What about an online webinar audience? The above questions apply, but the digital world suggests some additional ones need consideration. How many in your virtual audience are

- Elementary teachers?
- Middle school teachers?
- High school teachers?
- Sick and tired of webinars and attending only because it's required?
- Viewing the webinar on a smartphone in a car?
- Viewing the webinar on a laptop in their home?
- Viewing the webinar on a large screen with others in a schoolroom?
- From a school with a very different makeup than yours?

How many have

- Another screen open?
- Distractions as they watch (kids, pets, television, smartphone)?
- Muted their mics and turned off the camera?
- Found where the chat box is?
- Found the digital way to raise hands and send emojis?
- Used a breakout room before?

Again, as we will discuss in Chapter 2, the answers to these questions are more important than they might seem.

What to do when the audience is less familiar

It doesn't matter if your audience will be one person or many: you'll benefit from getting a sense of who they are before you address them.

It is one thing to do this when your audience is composed of people you work with every day, but how do you tackle the challenge when the audience is less familiar?

First, **consider what little you may know**—even if it's just generalities or decently informed assumptions. For example, as a principal, I may not know all the parents at Back-to-School Night, but I sort of do. I have done Back-to-School Nights before. If I've been at the school for a while, I can guess the parents' average age, average income level, and the percentage of them who have other children enrolled at the school. I can be pretty sure they aren't that familiar with education jargon. Similarly, as a consultant heading to a middle school in Florida, I don't know the teachers I'll be talking with, but I do have some experience with middle schools and middle school teachers, and I can assume that some features are similar to those of the middle school in Colorado where I once taught. Let experience be your starting place.

In some cases, you'll go in knowing almost nothing. What then?

Be inquisitive. Ask questions of people who might know about your audience, such as the principal of the school where you'll be speaking. Ask about the neighborhood and the school community. Maybe even ask for specific names you might use in a story. ("I know that Kelly is the department chair in the social studies department. That means Kelly knows how hard it is . . .").

Be observant. If you're going to a new school, consider driving around the neighborhood first to get a sense of it and the people who live there. Once at the venue, scan the room and notice the audience. How many look enthused to be there? Who is wearing team logo gear? Who has long hair? Who are the talkative ones? Who is hiding in the back? Some of these examples may strike you as trivial (long hair? logo wear?), but remember that even the trivial can be important.

Find out on the fly. Never forget that you can just simply ask for information as you speak: "Do you all have experience with ____?" or "Let me get a sense of where we are. If you are totally comfortable with this program, hold up five fingers; if you know nothing about it, hold up a fist. Hold up one, two, three, or four fingers as appropriate." Audiences hate being talked down to ("We already know this") and equally hate feeling lost ("Are we supposed to know this?").

Applying What You've Learned

Having done the work of audience analysis, effective speakers factor this information into their planning, adjusting their presentation style to fit the situation just as they might adjust their clothing choices for different occasions or weather forecasts. I changed clothes between the school day and coming back to meet parents at Back-to-School Night. I adjusted my speaking style, too. Talking to 6th graders is not the same as talking to the parents of 6th graders. Speakers can and should purposefully alter vocabulary, messaging, and manner to suit the audience they have. I am not suggesting that you become someone you aren't, but rather that you develop and employ tailored versions of your oral communication.

One of my former principals, Bryan, really knew how to apply audience analysis in working with staff. I remember showing up to a faculty meeting in February to see that Bryan had brought in a couple of performers from a local improv club. The idea was nice, right? The school year gets pretty draggy in February, and why not have a little fun? But I know what you're thinking: would everyone have fun playing improv games and getting up on stage? Might some not be in the mood for that? Might some feel stress at having to perform?

Bryan had thought these issues through in advance, considering what he knew about us, who the introverts and extroverts were, and who was struggling with issues at home. "I want to lighten things up because we are at the time of year when things seem a bit heavy," he explained. "I realize that we are in different places, so there is no pressure here. If you feel like watching and not participating, that is fine. If you aren't in a playful mood right now, you have permission to go do what you need to do."

On another occasion, the district informed Bryan that a Response to Intervention trainer would be available Friday afternoon and asked him to call a staff meeting. It was legal for the district to do this (students were dismissed at 3:15 p.m., and our contract hours required us to work until 4:15 p.m.), but Bryan knew what the district didn't: that none of the sports team coaches would be available to attend, that many teachers would not be in a receptive mood at the end of a long week, and that there were three teachers with young children who had arranged to start early and leave early to better handle their childcare schedules. He convinced the district to schedule the training at a different time. This and the get-out-of-improv option were both simple actions Bryan took based on understanding the audience. In the staff's minds, however, they were powerful demonstrations of thoughtfulness.

Michael Pinto is the principal of James Cole Elementary School in Indiana. He offers this idea:

> A big adjustment that is too often overlooked is "The Cheerleader Effect." Most people think that the "rah-rah" person is someone everyone wants. However, the room is half-full of extroverts who feed on that energy and the need to move around and meet others. The other half of the room is filled with introverts who wither and wilt at these moments. Allowing an opt-out for those in the introvert category is a move that is too often overlooked.

Meghan Everette is an educator in Utah and a director at the State Board of Education. She talks about using what you know to soften your message and applies this wisdom to coaching situations in a district where past leaders had tended to present initiatives as "do this now" demands. Here's an explanation in Meghan's own words:

> There were practices we really wanted to put forward, but just being directive wouldn't be a good move. So, we made adjustments to help lead them to the practice through understanding, and we would soften language around what was expected—lots of little changes that would ease anxiety and calm fears about the math overlords forcing something new.

How often have you seen the "overlords" problem leading to a resistant staff? That is always the result when we fail to understand the audience and adjust the message for them.

What about other types of talks? Each audience is unique, so each talk—even on the same topic—must be unique. Some of the adjustments needed will be clear to you when you think "audience first." For example:

- When leading professional development, if you know the average age of the audience is 30-something, don't use a reference only the over-50 crowd would get. Come up with a reference they likely *will* get.
- When talking to students, change your vocabulary and speaking pattern depending on the age of the students you are addressing.
- Don't feel compelled to use formal language because you feel it's expected of you as a leader. If colloquial language will better match the language of the listeners, support more effective communication, and be natural for you, go ahead and use it.
- If tech is your thing and you're presenting on technology, remind yourself that there will be some in your audience who are not as enthusiastic about incorporating digital tools or can be easily overwhelmed by them. Go slow and always circle back to the objective of supporting student learning.
- Avoid education jargon and acronyms or explain them if you need to. If a large majority of your audience doesn't know PLC, MTSS, EOG, ACES, SEL, EOY, AMI, CFAs DEI, and RTI, make sure to clarify what these abbreviations and acronyms mean.
- Don't explain jargon if you don't need to! If a large majority of your audience already knows what the above alphabet soup means, don't take up their time with definitions.
- Significant adjustments may be needed when addressing parents whose first language isn't English. Work to eliminate the frustrations they might experience while trying to understand. Change pacing, avoid idioms, and provide multiple ways to receive the message.
- Recognize your strengths and weaknesses in the content of your message and be prepared to do a little homework. For example, if you are new to leading a middle school, study the middle school math standards before meeting with the math department.
- Capitalize on opportunities to learn more about your audience. When walking through the hallway or running into someone in the

lunchroom, greet them, recall what you know about their personal life, listen, and respond with empathy and with individual concern. Connections built now will support future communication.
- Pay attention to how your audience feels in the moment and think about whether it is how you *want* them to feel.
- Think about what your listeners need to be successful in receiving your message. That may involve adjusting your timing, your language, and aspects of the presentation format and space.

In the Preface, I mentioned that the principles of speaking presented in this book are not just for official education leaders. Think about how making audience analysis available to your colleagues would benefit the entire staff. What if your building security personnel and office staff had audience awareness at the top of their minds? *Who is that person coming through the door? What are these parents thinking? How can I design my conversation with them to be most effective?* I am not suggesting that the customer is always right; they aren't. But they do have a perspective that can be understood and honored. I recall an elementary school nurse saying to a parent, "I understand, but she has a temperature of 102 degrees, and staying in class is not what's best for her. She really needs to be home getting better so she can return to school soon. It must be very hard on you because you have to get to work. I was in the same place last month with my son." She didn't start with what she wanted to say—*Pick up this sick child immediately!*—but rather with what the parent might be able to hear. What if all staff were versed in understanding and honoring others' perspectives?

The Simple Takeaway

It's not just about you. You don't speak in a vacuum. As a school leader, you can successfully avoid most communication problems if you spend purposeful time thinking about listeners before and as you craft your messages. Whether you are leading a staff or facilitating professional development or speaking at a retirement dinner or talking to the board or chatting with a staff member in the parking lot, always begin by understanding your audience.

Application Exercises

Exercise 1

Look back at the case study earlier in the chapter (p. 12). I think a mistake was made—one that could have been avoided if the audience had been considered carefully. In this case, the principal lost the respect of half of the students. Consider these questions:

- What key features of the audience did Jeannie fail to recognize?
- What would you have wanted to hear if you had been in the second audience?
- How would a better understanding of the audience have helped Jeannie avoid the mistake?
- How would you have created your message differently after analyzing the audience?

Exercise 2

List all the audiences you will be speaking to in the next two weeks—a PLC, a department meeting, the board of education, a school assembly, a teacher who wants to address a concern, a parent group—every talk you will be making. (Refer back to Steven Weber's lists on pp. 4–6 for a refresher.) Describe each audience in as much detail as you can; go ahead and make the lists long! A sample set of audience analytics for a Back-to-School Night address might be as follows:

- 75 percent female and 25 percent male
- Ages range from 25 to 40
- Parents of 5-year-old students, parents of 11-year-old students
- Most have more than one child at the school
- Most work full-time
- Some have a first language that is not English
- Primarily high school educated, with a few college graduates
- Lower to middle income
- From many different cultures
- Unfamiliar with educational terms and common acronyms (e.g., SEL, PLCs, PBL, DEI)

Now look at your own lists.

- How should you adjust your talk, knowing what you now know?
- What might you say that you wouldn't have thought of saying had you not made your lists?
- How does the way you design your messages change from one audience to the next?

2

What You Should Say

In many situations, your message's content is largely nonnegotiable. If you're presenting a new schedule or a new assessment, for example, you'll cover how the schedule will run and how the new assessment works. But there is much more to effective speaking than just putting the information out there; your goal is communicating *with* the audience. And although you're definitely responsible for what you say to listeners, you're also responsible for what the listeners understand. In this chapter, we'll dig into how to craft messages that include the essential content *and* do so in a way increases the odds it will be received and understood as intended.

Zero in on the Key Message

What do you need to say?

Notice that I didn't ask, "What do you *want* to say?" Most speakers have a lot that they want to say, and that's why most speakers say too much. They lose focus, they ramble, they include nonessential details. "Create an outline" is common advice when it comes to planning a talk, but before you do that, write down in one sentence exactly what your goal is. What are you hoping to achieve with this communication? What are audience members supposed to walk away knowing or doing or feeling? What should parents get from your talk? What should staff get from this meeting? What should this teacher get from your conference? What action should the school board take? You get the idea. Or, looking at it another way, what outcome would both you and your listener(s) regard as successful?

Yes, it can be a compound sentence. For example:

I want all teachers to understand the importance of teaching speaking skills, to understand the framework for making effective talks, and to learn practical activities they can use to develop student voices.

Reading includes much more than ink-on-paper reading, and reading teachers need to include specific instruction about how to read digital materials.

Parents will understand how our counselors support social and emotional learning and how to help their children get the support they need.

Kim will learn how certain behaviors disrupt relationships with other teachers and will use a performance improvement plan to monitor those behaviors.

The superintendent will see the need for 2.5 more full-time employees at my school and will authorize funding for those positions.

Students will be inspired to support our magazine sale fundraising efforts.

Decide the Scope of Your Message: Bite, Snack, or Meal?

Once you have your thesis statement, you can begin to add. But *how much* should you add? You have done the preliminary work of analyzing your audience, right? Given who they are and what you have to communicate, what will benefit them most? Do they need just a little bit of information, something more detailed, or comprehensive coverage of a topic?

I often see speakers serving meal-sized, comprehensive talks to people who only came for a snack. *But there is a whole meal's worth of information!* you say. OK, but that doesn't matter if your audience isn't going to swallow it. *Still,* you insist, *all the information is good information!* Yes, and the dessert my wife ordered was delicious and she insisted that I try it, but I was too full to want even a single forkful.

To be sure, there will be differences within the audience, whatever size or type of audience it is. A few people at a meeting, for example, probably *do* want the whole meal. We've all been in meetings where somebody kept asking questions, oblivious to how badly the majority wanted to move on. It's good to be prepared to offer more to appease those folks—just not at the expense of the majority's time. In Chapter 3, we'll look at ways to address their needs, including sharing information digitally.

When it comes to determining how much message to offer, many of us go first to the amount of time we need to fill. We think of 45-minute faculty meetings, 90-minute conference sessions, the 30 minutes allotted to Rotary Club speakers, the PD workshop that is scheduled for 6.5 hours to qualify for continuing education credits, and so on. Under no circumstances should you ever go *over* that time limit! But under many circumstances, you should feel free to use less time than is available. Gary Larson, creator of The Far Side cartoon, knows why. He once drew a student character in a classroom asking, "Mr. Osborne, may I be excused? My brain is full." Keep that cartoon in mind as you create your talk or presentation.

Refine Your Message

When we need to focus a message, we often start with the wrong question: "Is this information important?" If we believe that it is, we include it in our talk. But after reading Chapter 1, you can anticipate my response to that question: *important to whom?* You and your audience may have different ideas about what is important. A better question would be "Is this information going to have a positive impact on the listeners?" Will getting the information positively affect job performance, relationship building, motivation and encouragement, or some other category? With the "positive impact" filter, it is easier to critique your content and determine which of three categories it fits in: Must Include, Could Include, and Don't Include. (The Don't Include category is complicated and needs a lot of unpacking; we'll explore it further in Chapter 3.)

The kind of content that falls in each of these categories is usually context specific. As examples, the leader of a PLC "must include" norms for how the group will run and a calendar for task completion; a workshop leader "must include" the schedule of the day, explanations of how the planned interactive activities will work, and ways to assess the learning, among other things. I encourage you to consult resources such as *The Effective Facilitator's Handbook* (Toll, 2023) or *Training Design, Delivery, and Diplomacy* (Young & Osborne, 2023) for help becoming a more successful facilitator or trainer. Remember that this book is sharing ideas that work for *all* speaking situations. I will talk generically about what typically qualifies as Must-Include information and show how that thinking applies universally, and I'll do that with a made-up scenario.

Assume that I have been asked to give a conference presentation on how to improve the oral communication skills of all students. This is great, because I have lots of content about oral communication, including the following:

1. The history of oral communication in education: how it has been part of the official curriculum in the past but is seldom taught these days
2. My history as a speaker, including my days in high school forensics and debate and my collegiate debate experience
3. The top speaking skills employers want in prospective employees
4. How learning to be a competent, confident communicator helps students' self-esteem
5. How improved oral communication improves reading

6. The framework for creating a talk: the five elements students must consider before they speak
7. The framework for delivering a talk: the six elements students must consider as they speak
8. How students spoke in my class when I started teaching: the story of the first book reports I heard in my elementary classroom
9. How to incorporate speaking activities into all curricular areas
10. How to incorporate speaking activities into all grade levels
11. The real meaning of student voice and how speaking well is the key to student advocacy
12. The lack of instructional resources focused on teaching speaking and how speaking activities are an afterthought in other units
13. Current rubrics for scoring speaking and how they miss the mark
14. How to use rubrics based on my speaking framework's 11 elements and how they help all students
15. Current classroom activities that involve speaking and how those fail to develop better skills
16. How teachers treat teaching speaking differently from teaching writing
17. Perceptions about speaking and how the fear of public speaking keeps us from teaching students
18. Different types of speaking: formal and informal; one-to-one, small group, large group; in-person and digital/remote
19. Specific skills needed to be a good speaker and how to evaluate speakers
20. Examples of strong student speeches after specific lessons
21. Examples of weak student speeches without specific lessons
22. Examples of great orators and poor orators
23. Digital tools that can be used to showcase and teach speaking
24. How to modify speaking for digital presentations
25. Lessons for teaching students how to master each of the 11 elements of creating and delivering talks
26. How to support introverts/reluctant speakers

In short, speaking is a topic I know very well and could go on about for quite a while. But let's look at that list again in light of a one-sentence statement about my speaking objective:

I want all teachers to understand the importance of teaching speaking, to understand the framework for making effective talks, and to learn practical activities they can use to develop student voices.

With that in mind, what are my Must Includes? Which items on the list will accomplish my first goal, conveying the importance of teaching speaking? Probably Items 3, 4, 5, and 11. Which accomplish my second goal, explaining the framework for all talks? Items 6 and 7. And which accomplish the third goal, teaching practical activities? Items 14 and 25. If I have 60 or 90 minutes to talk at a conference, that's all I'll include.

But what if I have a half-day workshop's worth of time? What additional information could I include with this additional time—information that would be appreciated and well-received by my audience? I've found that teachers are interested in my history (2, 8), in examples of before and after student talks (20, 21), and in how to teach speaking in all subjects and at all grade levels (9, 10). Full-day workshops allow time to explore how current practices miss the mark (12, 13, 15), to demonstrate digital tools that showcase and teach speaking (23), to explain adjusting talks for digital presentations (24), and to show how to encourage reluctant speakers to talk (26).

Finally, what should I just not include? Well, I've learned that audiences are seldom that interested in the history of oral communication. It's information that doesn't seem to have much applicability to what needs to be done in the classroom today.

I recommend using this three-part filtering process for all your talks. For example, if you have prepared a slide deck, look at the Slide Sorter view. What slides cannot be removed without undermining your message? What slides could be taken out if you get word that your 30 minutes has been cut to 15? What slides could be cut right now without altering your message in a real way or affecting your objective?

If you'll be addressing your school's PTCO, go ahead and list all the topics you could speak about and prioritize them: *These five items must be talked about; if time permits, I could say something about these three; and, realistically, the rest could be cut out and no one would care.*

More about Must Includes

This category covers both the message's most important point, as you would expect, and procedural techniques, which you might not—aspects of a message like employing meaningful organization, connecting to the audience, and including essential information, positives, and time for audience response and reflection.

The main point

Remembering the goal of sharing ideas applicable to all speaking situations, let's start with some basics: *say what you are supposed to say.* There is often a mismatch between the speaker's purpose and what the speaker actually delivers. Even leaders who write down the main idea sometimes veer off topic and fail to include it in the talk they're giving or meeting they're conducting.

Keith Young is an education writer and trainer and a former principal, teacher, and staff developer. Asked about communication mistakes that he sees leaders make, he commented that a big problem is "being too indirect." Indeed, the main point may not even appear. Here he is, talking about a middle school principal who needed to correct a 7th grade teacher:

> [The teacher] needed to be focused on the curriculum, which is a pretty basic thing, but sometimes what teachers are focusing on is not even closely related to the standards. This principal talked to the teacher for about 40 minutes, and I scripted the whole conversation. He never once told her to stop doing the outside-the-curriculum activity that she was doing, even though that was the main point of the meeting. Afterward, he asked me, "How'd I do?" I said, "You never told her to stop." He said, "Sure I did." I showed him the notes. He thought he had been direct, but he hadn't.

Keith offered a second example of the omitting-the-key-point problem, telling me about how he had accompanied his nephew to a middle school welcome session for incoming 6th graders. There was a student band playing outside the school and a different student band playing inside. A student chorus sang before the assembly started, and two student speakers spoke. ("They weren't good speakers," Keith noted dryly, reinforcing my belief that we shortchange speaking in schools.) He continued:

> Then the administrators got up to speak. They had a PowerPoint presentation, and they kept talking about how the school was all about relationships. Then they flipped through the slides, spending 90 seconds talking about the academics and 30 minutes talking about discipline. They told us basically nothing about learning and that they were really focused on classroom management, which made me think there must be a lot of behavior issues here. They said many times that they were all about relationships, but they didn't tell us much about themselves or seem interested in learning about us. I left thinking that "relationships" was just a buzz phrase with no real connection to the school's actual priorities.

In this case, there was a mismatch between the stated main point (the school values relationships) and the main point as the audience heard it (the school has discipline problems). The administrators included a main point all right (behavior) but failed to label it as such. Audiences aren't fooled easily. They correctly believe that what speakers spend the most time talking about is what matters most to those speakers. They can often identify the main point even if the speaker seems not to.

Staying on message has another advantage: it allows you to be confident in uncomfortable situations. Imagine an instructional coach with a background as an English language arts teacher who needs to work with a difficult math teacher. If the math teacher succeeds in making the conversation about math, the coach will feel out of his element, and the math teacher will think, "He has no idea about my subject matter or the math standards." If the coach keeps the main point in mind (e.g., improving behavior management, student engagement, equity, or something else universal to all teachers), and if the coach speaks only about that topic, he can be successful.

Meaningful organization

While we all know that organization is important, sometimes organizational elements are shortchanged when it comes time to plan a talk.

What are the elements of a well-organized talk, anyway? We ask teachers to organize their lessons with anticipatory sets, guided practice, and checks for understanding or some other system, but do we give much attention to *our* organization? All talks—even small and informal ones—benefit from applying good organizational ideas.

First, there should be **an introduction**—an opening that grabs your listeners' attention and excites them about what is to come. It's true that some messages from education leaders are data dumps, simply because there's lots of information to share. In that case, you want an opening that clarifies your purpose is to convey information. Most talks are *not* data dumps, however. In those cases, it's necessary to create engagement early—ideally within the first 30 seconds. This is where you want to set the tone for your talk and convince your audience that they need to pay attention.

A new principal once came to me seeking advice. At the beginning of the school year, she had decided to open every faculty meeting with kudos. She created a form teachers could fill out extolling the virtues of a colleague and the wonderful thing that colleague had done. The principal then read these statements of praise and gratitude at the beginning of each meeting. The idea became very popular—so popular, in fact, that reading the kudos started to take most of the time scheduled for the meeting, which is why she approached me for advice. I suggested that she randomly select three each week from all the forms put into the Kudos Box and post the rest online in a Kudos tab. (See Chapter 3 for more about how to move in-person items online.) I don't know if the kudos fad wore off, but I hope not. Opening a meeting with the message that attendees are valued is a great idea. Creating an atmosphere where people want to be is important. For that reason, I never use icebreakers. Remember that one-third to one-half of your audience are introverts, as I am. We aren't thrilled about being at the meeting or in the professional development session in the first place, and the first thing you make us do is some forced get-to-know-you activity? Awkward. Let us get to know each other when it becomes important to do so, like during a group activity integral to the purpose of the session.

Do you have a tight organizational structure with **clear transitions** from one topic or section to the next? In my book *Well Spoken: Teaching Speaking to All Students* (Palmer, 2011), I refer to signposts. Just as you always know where you are as you drive down a highway (Limon: 57 miles; Limon: 33 miles; Limon: Next exit), listeners should know where they are in your talk. For example:

> *OK, team, we're only going to spend 10 minutes on this, but it is important to understand what the legal ramifications are to the new law about LGBTQ+ materials in classrooms. Next, we'll spend 20 minutes in grade-level groups discussing what changes, if any, need to be made. Finally, we'll share our concerns about the new law. First, then, the legal ramifications and potential problems for teachers.*

Returning to restate your structure at appropriate transition points helps to tie the pieces together. So, for example, you might say:

> *Now that we understand the legal aspect, let's get into groups for the change discussion....*

> *OK, this is tough for some of us. I know we don't all agree. Let's share concerns....*

Michael Pinto reminds us of another great organizational tool, **repetition of a key idea**:

> I heard a leader present to a school board a passionate plea to "Protect Our Assets." Three words. Spoken eloquently. Spoken, then respoken throughout the speech. It resonates still as I recite it. Find your phrase. Speak it. Revisit it. Drive it home.

You can imagine that the talk included several "assets"—perhaps students, perhaps district reputation, perhaps facilities—but coming back to the simple, overarching theme had power that stayed with him to this day. A brilliant content move.

Steven Weber has noticed that even educators who have obviously planned their message tend to ramble when they get to the closing. Do *you* always have **a well-thought-out ending**? The simplest might be to restate the one sentence that explained the purpose of the meeting. Summarize the key points of the session, meeting, or talk. Some talks should end with a call for action; some with a heartfelt thank-you; some with an inspirational story; some with restatement of the next steps to take. Avoid rambling and avoid "Oh, looks like our time is up. Bye."

"Connectors"

If you think about what great communicators do, you'll notice that their talks always include comments that connect themselves and their topic to their listeners. For them, there is no "generic talk." Yes, I share the very same framework for teaching speaking no matter where I talk, but the presentation is different in Shoreline, Washington, than it is in Riyadh, Saudi Arabia. I add what I call *connectors*.

The first kind of connector to consider are the **words and phrases that connect the content of your message to the lives and concerns of the listeners**. They answer the audience's question, "Why is this message relevant to *me*?" For example, occasionally educators enrolled in one of my workshops wonder aloud why they need to be there. "Teaching speaking? That's for English teachers, right? I teach science."

In introductory remarks during a "How to Teach Speaking" workshop, I might point out that students talk in every class and every subject. This point is a connector. Are there class discussions? They will be better—deeper, more illuminating—if students speak well. Are there lab reports or presentations of any kind? They will be clearer and more engaging if students speak well. Do students collaborate on some assignments? Teaching speaking across the subject areas is a way to develop and reinforce skills that are widely useful.

Like I just did in the paragraph prior, work into your message explicit statements underscoring how what you are talking about will positively impact your listeners. Don't assume that audience members will make these connections on their own. And, of course, if the content *doesn't* actually affect the listeners, either it doesn't belong in your message or there are audience members who do not need to receive that message and should be excused (see Chapter 1).

The second kind of connector to think about are the **aspects of a message that create a link between yourself and the listeners**. They answer the audience's question, "Why should I trust this speaker's take or advice?" Establishing credibility is important for all speakers, especially when they are likely to be seen as "outsiders." And that is how education leaders are often perceived—as the Them to the Us. Think of a staff developer from the district office; a principal who isn't in the classroom; a teacher who doesn't understand the pressure a parent is under; a board member who represents a geographic subset of district residents; a consultant brought in to teach a new assessment technique. These gaps exist, and a speaker's choice of words can bridge them. Theresa Stager, principal at Saline High School in Michigan, puts it this way:

> The best leaders I have seen speak professionally can connect their messages to the mass. It could be in small sections of the presentation that connect to different groups, or by relating the message to something that affects the entire audience (COVID-19, teenagers, parenting, etc.).

Let me give an example. Mary was the superintendent of my district for a number of years. When she visited schools, she always sought ways to establish connections with the people she met. Remember the list of trivial seeming questions related to learning about your audience (see pp. 15–16)? Mary used them.

Erika, hello. Wasn't your hair longer when I last visited? I love the new look.

Ah, a Broncos jersey, eh? Are you a fan, too? I was so disappointed this season. Do you think the new coach will help?

Tim, how are your boys doing? They were on the basketball team here, right?

How did the school carnival go? I remember that last year all the goldfish died before you could sell them.

Wow, this classroom looks different from the 3rd grade classroom I had. It was all chalkboards in my day!

With just a few thoughtful words, Mary went from a Big Deal Administrator to a friend, someone who knew what it was like in our shoes. People liked having Mary visit—not typical in my experience; superintendent visits were usually high-stress and unwelcome. Also notice the variety of connectors Mary used. There was a fashion comment, a sports comment, a parenting comment, a story specifically for this school, a teaching comment—something for everyone in the audience to relate to.

I don't have Mary's facility for remembering names and details, so I carry a notebook. Immediately after I leave a place, I jot down notes—Dan, wrestling coach; Katie, recovering from back surgery; Aaron, worried a lot about over testing; magazine fundraiser is starting—everything I can think of that I might be able to use as connectors when I return.

I also use the notebook before I arrive to make notes about the community and the school. Then I can toss in comments like "How long is that construction on Peoria Avenue going to last? That has to make your drive tougher." Or "What we are discussing today fits in well with this part of your school motto that I noticed when I walked in." Or "The Panthers! My high school mascot was a panther, too." These additions to your message bring you closer to your listeners and make them more likely to attend to what you are saying.

Contrast Mary's approach with that of the principal at the first school where I taught, who loved to say, "*I don't have ulcers, but I'm a carrier!*" She thought that line was hilarious and repeated it often. I thought it was a foolish thing to say. What I heard was "I'm a jerk, I don't care that I'm a jerk, and I'll make your life miserable." I heard, "I'm fine with damaging staff morale." A connecter is what good leaders use to bridge the gap between speaker and listener; it's not words that draw attention to the gap or make it wider.

Michael Pinto uses stories to connect with listeners. He suggests using "personal examples that include failures, failures overcome" or "self-deprecating" stories. In his words, "They make you more real to the audience and give you credibility. A story told well sticks. With it, so does your message." Note Michael's emphasis on removing the perception of superiority sometimes associated with his position. Leaders, especially new leaders, sometimes believe that they must appear infallible, strong, and powerful to command respect. Michael knows that great leaders avoid that mindset. Include content that makes you approachable and relatable to your listeners.

Positives

When I started teaching, I bought a multipack of red pens. I knew that teachers used red pens to mark papers; as a language arts teacher, I would be assigning and grading many essays, so I'd need those pens.

I was diligent, never missing a student mistake. Misspelling? Circled in red. Run-on sentence? Underlined in red. No paragraph? A big red backward double *P*. I went through a lot of red pens. So many things wrong, so much to fix—how discouraging for my students, right? It was a while before I stopped focusing entirely on the errors and started considering the bigger picture of my students' essays and talents. Eventually, I bought a multipack of green pens and started highlighting great parts of the papers, too.

I thought of this experience a lot when Janet was my principal. Every staff member knew that when you saw Janet coming down the hall, she was coming to tell someone, or maybe all of us, that There Was a Problem. "Uh-oh, here comes Janet" was a common refrain, and we wondered which one of us was going to be in trouble. In the three years that Janet was the principal, I can't recall receiving a single compliment from her, and I assure you that I did at least *one* good thing during those three years.

There are different ideas about how many positives it takes to outweigh one negative. Some say three positives, some say five, some say seven. A study of leadership teams at a large information processing company discovered that the members of the highest-performing teams heard six positives for every one negative (Zenger & Folkman, 2013). The specific number varies, but everyone agrees that it takes *multiple* positives to offset a negative. We seemed to be wired to react more strongly to bad comments than to good ones. You probably recognize this in your life and have spent time dwelling on one parent complaint while completely forgetting about the several parents who expressed how happy they were with your leadership.

For leaders, the ratio of positive expressions of support to negative complaints is horribly askew. Unfortunately, to be successful at leading others, you must remember to recognize success. To be clear, you do not have to be responsible for all the positives: "I have to talk to Erik about doing a better job monitoring his students in the hallway, so I need to say six nice things first." Positives can come from teammates, parents, and others. You do need to contribute some, and you do need to create a culture where positives are the norm. Keep your "green pen" handy.

Case Study

It was the evening of the 4th grade performance. After weeks of rehearsal, the students are ready to present the Lewis and Clark story before an assembly of their families. Several different Lewises and Clarks were ready to deliver a few lines each, and then the entire 4th grade would sing a few songs. The parents were settled in, the students were on the risers, and the principal, Suzanne, came to the microphone:

> *Good evening, everyone. Welcome. Before we get started, I just wanted to say a few words. First, I want to thank you for supporting last month's school carnival. It was a big success. We were able to raise enough money to buy some new swings for our playground. Some of you who have been around the school for a while know that we had to remove some of the old swings for safety reasons. The new swings should be here within a month. We'll keep our fingers crossed. I want to thank the PTCO volunteers who helped us, including the two chairpersons, Margie Lacy and Lynn Carmona. Margie and Lynn aren't here tonight, but they did a lot of hard work. We really appreciate their efforts. We will be looking for volunteers for next year's carnival, so think about it.*
>
> *Anyhow, the 4th graders have been working very hard on this show. They have been studying explorers this year as part of the 4th grade curriculum, and our music teacher, Ms. Diaz, found this wonderful show. We love to be able to integrate specials into regular class units. So here you go.*
>
> Ms. Diaz came to the microphone and said, "Without further ado, our 4th grade show!" The pianist began playing, and the students started to sing the opening song.

Time for response and reflection

As noted, leaders are familiar with crisis mode. They get into a mindset where, in the interest of time, they want to fly in, fix it, and move on. Unfortunately, that approach tends not to produce the best long-term results. Avoid talking *at* listeners. It is all too common for a speaker to show up, talk *at* the audience, and leave. Chapter 1 again: *It isn't just about you.* You need to let others process and contribute. This applies whether speaking one-on-one or speaking to larger groups.

Keith Young talked to me about the need for allowing input in one-on-one situations. When he works with coaches, too often he sees coaches who believe "me telling a teacher what to do" is a coaching conversation. In Keith's opinion, the "let me tell you how to fix it" mindset is like "coming in with a hammer" when brainstorming is what's needed. Processing with the teacher or helping them reflect is much more productive.

Amy Illingworth is an assistant superintendent and author. She made the same point about speaking to a small group and pointed out that speakers must be careful to avoid overrunning the audience. Reinforcing my idea that talking *at* the audience is inappropriate, she offers a suggestion for better talk *with* the audience:

> Allow time for participants to reflect, dialogue, or get up for a connection activity that ties the work to the humans. Provide links for future study/resources to refer back to later.

Note Amy's mentioning the need to connect to the audience or, in her words, to provide "ties" between the information presented and the human beings who will be called on to do something with this information. And note that she edits the message for maximum relevance by preparing links to additional content.

Michael Pinto put it this way:

> One of the biggest adjustments that occurs in the professional settings where I see speakers is to find the balance to "process." There is a need to avoid the constant "sit and get." There is also a need to be intentional with the timing and frequency of "turn and talk." When new information is being presented, there is a need to allow more processing and question/answer time, along with "work time," if that fits the bill.

A cautionary note: monitor responses and be prepared to take action as needed. Processing and reflection can quickly degenerate into something unproductive. From Meghan Everette:

> Sometimes people start fighting when they don't realize the limitations of the meeting. For example, people would complain to me as a math

coach that they didn't like or think the formative testing system was fair. But in a PLC, we couldn't do anything to change that. What we could do was come up with strategies to attack the problems and write up our issue with specific questions to submit to the math department. Knowing those parameters and setting expectations helps. If teachers were left to discuss on their own, they would say we should get rid of the tests altogether, but the reality was they didn't have authority or sway over that, nor was that what the meeting was for.

Turn and talk and reflection prompts need to be on point. Allow time for processing. but keep that processing focused. Set parameters. Here's an example:

> *Discuss how the assessment changes will affect what you do now, then brainstorm ideas for implementing those changes at your grade level. It is not possible to pretend that the changes don't exist, and venting displeasure won't move us forward. How can we make this work?*

Advice for Troublesome Situations

All of the speaking occasions mentioned so far are relatively safe ones: meeting new parents, visiting schools, coaching, leading a PLC. Sometimes the occasion for speaking is trickier. What type of content is needed then? What must be included, could be included, and should not be included when leaders have to address problematic issues and tough audiences? Let's explore ways to navigate those waters.

Uncomfortable content

There is no way to avoid uncomfortable content. No one likes being corrected, but sometimes correction is necessary. No one likes having their ideas rejected, but some ideas deserve rejection. Few people enjoy changes to established routines, but continuous improvement requires shaking up the status quo.

Many talks that school leaders give are critical or corrective in nature and include messages that are not easy to deliver. Occasionally, parents and staff must be told that their opinions will not prevail. Frequently, talks introduce new requirements that may not sit well at first. You don't always have happy, lovable messages, but you want to maintain healthy relationships. How can we make the unpleasant acceptable? How can we prepare to deliver messages that listeners won't love?

Steven Weber believes that when there is a specific message to convey, "winging it" is not an option:

> My first strategy is "writing a script" to prepare my talking points. What are the three or four points that I want to share with the person during the conversation? This strategy helps me focus on the points that need to be made and helps eliminate the emotions that go along with an uncomfortable meeting.

Meghan Everette believes the script should contain "facts, specificity, and radical transparency":

> One, you come with the *facts*. If you are going to try and talk to someone where a change is needed—be it in practice, management, or another area—you need to have data. Just a generalized "Your students' scores aren't great" or "Kids are off task" isn't going to get it done. What is the goal and how far off is that goal? "Eighty-five percents of kids at your grade level are on reading level; the number in your class is 63 percent." Or "During my last observation, I counted seven children out of their seats in a 20-minute period." This leads to the second thing you need in a script—*specificity*. Using generalizations or unclear words isn't really helpful. It leads to people not knowing what they have done wrong (or right) or what they need to do to correct it. Clarity is a necessity. Both of these contribute to the third principle, *radical transparency*. You have to be honest about where you are, where you are going, and what has to change to get there. It does require a certain element of trust, but it also makes it possible to have these conversations. If a teacher is not being successful in some way, they probably already know it, and pussyfooting around the issue doesn't help.

In the situations Meghan mentions, your content should also provide support for the changes necessary. As she notes, the teacher may be aware of the problem but have no sense of how to fix it. Provide ideas and resources. In Keith Young's words,

Offer solutions. Instead of just pointing out the problem, suggest possible solutions or ask them how they think they could improve. This shows your intention to support their growth, not just criticize their actions.

Here is the advice Keith gives instructional coaches:

1. *Prepare for the conversation.* Identify the problem, gather all necessary facts, and think about what you want to convey and what outcome you hope to achieve.
2. *Begin the conversation on a positive note.* Recognize the individual's strengths and contributions. This helps to reassure the person that you value their work.
3. *Frame the issue as a challenge to be overcome, not as a personal flaw.* Use "I" statements to express your concern, such as "I have noticed that . . ." instead of "You always . . . ." This reduces the chances of the person feeling attacked.
4. *Be specific about the behavior that needs to change and avoid attributing it to the individual's personality.* Discuss the impact of the behavior on the team or the organization, so they understand why it's a problem.
5. *Listen and empathize.* Give them a chance to share their perspective. They might have reasons for their behavior that you weren't aware of. Showing empathy will make them more open to your feedback.

In situations where pushback will occur, it's helpful to script out every counterargument you think audience members may make and what you are going to say in response. Again, from Keith:

Do background research. Maybe you were a secondary teacher and are now an elementary principal not familiar with the kindergarten standards. Do a little homework before you have the conversation. This takes a bit of time, but it is empowering. "Oh yeah, I've thought through everything somebody could say." Overprepared leads to confidence.

Test out the script. In Steven Weber's words,

Find a close friend (in state or out of state) who will listen to the scenario. Share how you hope to address the conversation with your close friend. Practice your talking points. Ask for feedback.

Role-play with a mentor or trusted coworker. Ask if the message will be effective and if the warmth comes through. Modify what you plan to say based on the feedback you receive.

The preparation before talks on volatile subjects is a lot of work: choosing the three or four key concepts, researching, anticipating, and preparing answers for all possible challenges, figuring out to say it nicely, practicing, role-playing with a valued coworker . . . this is time-consuming, and if there is one thing you likely lack, it is time. When you realize that not all your preparation will end up being part of the talk—"I was prepared to say _____, but it didn't come up"—that may seem like time wasted. I have two responses to that. First, "I was prepared to say _____, but it didn't come up" is better than "Drat, I never thought of that, and I really floundered there." Second, I'll suggest a math problem: Would you rather spend one hour preparing for a tough talk or spend several hours cleaning up poor communication? Bear in mind that this cleanup might involve

- Having to make multiple talks because the issue wasn't solved the first time.
- Having to explain the message to confused listeners because they didn't get it.
- Needing to apologize for words that alienated the listeners.
- Being reprimanded by your superior for not solving the old problem or perhaps creating a new problem.
- Spending mental time being angry or frustrated with yourself.

The good news is that you will improve at going through the preparation process. You'll know the grade-level standards and issues. You'll know the listeners. You'll see the same arguments again and will have your counterarguments ready for reuse. You'll have a basket of strategies and resources to share as needed. You'll recognize that the current situation is like a past situation and can draw upon experience. You'll have defusing language and phrases ready. In sum, you will be more and more comfortable dealing with the uncomfortable.

Adjustments for explosive content

Critical race theory. LGBTQ+ issues. Diversity, equity, and inclusion efforts. Removing books from classrooms and libraries. Rewriting books to sanitize them for today's sensibilities. School vouchers.

As I write this, the environment is such that the mere mention of these terms causes upset. Lots of upset. I'd like to believe that future readers of this book will say, "Yeah, those used to be polarizing issues, and they created enormous, hate-filled arguments, but we are over it now." I'm afraid instead that new issues will be added to the list. Of course, while this list may be politically charged, there are perpetual education-related issues that also lead to very heated exchanges. Mention "phonics and reading" or suggest moving high school starting time back a couple of hours and see what happens. As I said earlier, there are landmines everywhere.

If there is a topic that is sensitive or may be offensive to some, you may want to announce the content beforehand and offer a preview—a trigger warning. Something that may seem innocuous to some can be upsetting to others, so much so that they will check out and miss critical aspects of learning. School counselor Gabrielle Price told me about a health teacher's food diary assignment and how students with disordered eating really struggled with it. Now in her school, students are told that the assignment is coming up and are given accommodations that are comfortable for them. Additionally, students get notice the day before some discussion topics are presented. Gabrielle knows that her school has survivors of sexual assault, and the school has lost students to suicide in the past. Before talks about consent or suicide prevention, students are notified and reminded that if attendance might be an issue for them, they should come speak to the counselor about their concerns. The idea is not to offer an opt-out but to figure out what the issue might be for the student and decide how to approach it. Forewarning like this will do a lot to reduce the number of calls from parents who are upset that their child came home upset. "This content is coming up, so please do what you need to do to prepare yourself" is a useful statement in many situations.

That kind of thinking doesn't just apply to students, does it? As a leader, you need to do the same kind of thinking to prepare your staff, teachers you coach, or other adults you interact with when tough content is on the table.

In instances where tough topics cannot be avoided, what can be done to mitigate problems? What content can lower the potential for emotions spinning out of control? Theresa Stager emphasizes listening first:

> Situations such as these are tough for both sides of the conversation. I look for the reason behind what the person's serious issue may be. Are they overprotective of something, and this is a reflection of that? Are they feeling attacked and need support? Is there a conflict that exists in another part of this situation that could be causing the issue? All behavior is communication. I begin by trying to understand, listening first, and creating an empathetic environment. When the other person shares where they are and what is happening, and I share what this issue has created for me, we can work together to solve it, decide what to do next, and know how to help this situation in the future.

Theresa's advice is modeled in a story about the aftermath of a prom after-party that had turned violent. Because of the sensitive nature of the topic, I won't identify the sender who shared this story with me.

> A father got a call from the hospital at 1:30 a.m. Sunday and was told his child had been shot and was in the emergency room. At first, he was frightened, but by Monday afternoon he was mad, and he wanted to visit the school and lash out at the one responsible—which, in this parent's eyes, was the school that permitted the prom after-party to happen.
>
> I was in the line of fire when the parent arrived. I met him in the main office, and we walked together to the School Counseling Services (SCS) office. There, the patient and well-trained counselor provided a master class on how to cool down a hostile situation. The counselor listened with a neutral expression, not interrupting as the angry parent bad-mouthed a host of school personnel. He ranted. He raved. He blustered

and threatened. I felt my blood pressure rising, but the counselor just listened calmly. Finally, the parent admitted how badly this whole incident had scared him. He confessed that he did not know how to help his recovering daughter or his suffering wife. Then he cried.

Throughout it all, the counselor did not waver. She did not overreact. She empathized with all of the parent's concerns. She admitted that she would have fallen apart in the same situation. She gave him tissues. She pledged support with this child's reentry into school and finally, she recommended the book *Thrivers* by Michele Borba.

I was extremely nervous, agitated, and on edge throughout this whole conversation. In a time where families, administrators, and teachers are needlessly adversarial, this was a wonderful example of how effective communicators can work together to rebuild positive relationships at our school.

The purpose of sharing this advice is two-fold: to remind you to listen well and to advise you to seek help in difficult situations. There may be people around you like the SCS counselor. And when it comes to dealing with highly charged political issues? Keith Young makes this vital point:

> Creating a message for a potentially explosive situation requires thoughtfulness, empathy, and strategic framing. It's essential to focus on the common ground, ensure all voices are heard, and promote a culture of respect.

Jessica Holloway, an innovation coach based in Tennessee, adds this:

> Crafting a message that addresses a controversial or sensitive topic requires precision and care. First, you have to ensure you know what you are saying is accurate. This may require research into local, state, or federal policies or laws. Knowing that the answer or decision is bound by external forces gives context and clarity on constraints, meaning you personally did not make the decision. It is also an opportunity to redirect the other person's energy toward how to advocate for change or elevate their voice in the appropriate setting or with the appropriate audience. Sometimes you will be the messenger; be sure you know the message.

Meghan Everette agrees:

Words have been politicized. Certain phrases can raise people's hackles because of how they interpret the words, so figuring out the right words to use when discussing what we want for kids and the importance of programs is a big deal. Understanding the different sides of an issue is key. You can't avoid a landmine that you don't know is there. Also talking from a perspective of what the various parties agree on is a good move. *We agree that kids need to read. We agree that kids need access to books in order to read. We agree kids should have some level of choice in their reading selections.* Just starting from a place of agreement is helpful. You can also just state, "Hey, we do not agree on the best way to reach our goal, but I do think we agree on the goal of having students succeed. Let's start with what else we do agree with." Understanding what each person desires to have happen or come out of the meeting is a good starting point. You can then set a reasonable expectation around what you can accomplish together.

Keith Young offers a checklist and uses incorporating LGBTQ+ content into English language arts courses as an example:

1. *Acknowledge the sensitivity.* Begin by acknowledging the sensitivity and the emotional significance of the topic. Recognizing this will demonstrate your understanding and respect for all viewpoints.
2. *Highlight shared goals.* Remind everyone about the shared goals and values that everyone in the room holds—the well-being, growth, and education of the students. This common ground can serve as a foundation for the discussion.
3. *Emphasize respect and understanding.* Reinforce the importance of respect and understanding in this discussion. Encourage everyone to listen to differing viewpoints with an open mind.
4. *State the facts.* Share the current research and professional guidelines related to LGBTQ+ literature in schools—for instance, including its potential benefits, such as promoting inclusivity, understanding, and empathy.
5. *Share the proposal.* Then, introduce the idea of integrating LGBTQ+ literature into the curriculum. Be clear that the proposal

is about creating an inclusive and diverse educational environment that respects and acknowledges all students' realities, including those who identify as LGBTQ+.
6. *Invite feedback.* Encourage everyone to share their thoughts and feelings about the proposal. Make it clear that all opinions are valued and will be considered in the decision-making process.
7. *Ensure safety.* If you know someone in the room has a particularly strong stance, consider speaking to them privately beforehand. Make sure they understand the importance of maintaining a respectful and safe discussion environment.
8. *Promote active listening.* Encourage participants to practice active listening—truly hearing and trying to understand each other's viewpoints, even if they don't agree.

Your responsibility as a leader is not to please everyone; it's to make decisions that are in the best interest of the education community you serve while respecting the dignity of all individuals involved. Some people will be angry, some full of hate, and some will, in their minds, lose. Be ready. Arrange for help. Who on your staff has experience defusing volatile situations as the counselor defused the after-prom situation? Who has been there, done that? What language do they use? What has worked in their experience? Learn from them. You don't have to do this alone.

The Content of Quick Conversations

I can't conclude this chapter without noting that leaders engage in lots of small talk, too. Most of the examples in this chapter come from formal talks—presentations to the school board, meeting with teachers, and talks where the stakes are high. Those can certainly have a huge impact on school culture and school image. You need to think carefully about what you should say. But little talks matter too. Keith Young puts it this way:

> It's vital to interact with everyone regularly, not just during meetings or official events. Casual conversations in the hallway, joining staff

for lunch, or dropping into classrooms can make you more accessible and relatable.

Michael Pinto agrees:

I was inspired today to write a message called "Dialogue with Meaning" today after two quick conversations. One was with a 2nd grade teacher who popped into my office during her prep period and asked if she could sit and read a few pages of notes. We talked about her son and her parenting, and it was real. It was also quick. But the dialogue stuck. The second conversation was with our music teacher, in the hallway right outside her classroom. She has had three very bad weeks in her personal life—the death of two pets and a musical setback outside school. Again—this conversation was real. Both conversations were still rattling in my head six hours later. These moments matter. The words leaders speak in moments can heal, or they can harm.

What do you say in the hallway to teachers? I had a principal who walked past teachers and never said a word. No "Hello, how are you?" No "Good morning." Nothing. What should you say to students as you walk by? "Looking good!" or "So glad you're here today." What should you say in the lunchroom? Business talk only, or should you share personal stories? What kind of relationship do you want to have with those you lead? That relationship is built as much in the small moments as in the large ones. What you choose to say in informal, casual conversation is as important as what you choose to say in big and formal presentations. It is possible that genuine caring for those you lead will increase engagement, effort, and loyalty. Genuine caring—not "I know I am supposed to be doing this so I will *seem* caring"—is the key here.

The Simple Takeaway

Whether your talk is formal or informal, to one person or several. or high-stakes or low-stakes, taking time to come up with the right things to say will make your life much easier. Always think about Must Includes, Could Includes, and Don't Includes before you craft a message.

Application Exercises

Exercise 1

The school district held a big kick-off event to start the new school year, with all the district's teachers—more than 2,000 people—assembled in the football stadium on the morning of the first day back from summer holiday. Inspiring music blared from the stadium speakers, balloons were everywhere, and teachers were wearing their school colors. It was an event. Jim, the superintendent, approached the microphone. Here's what he said:

> *Welcome! I am thrilled to see all of you and excited to start a new year with you. I know there are mixed feelings: some sadness at leaving summer behind, some apprehension about the new year, some excitement about new assignments.*
>
> *I also have mixed feelings. This summer, my sister passed away. She had been battling cancer for some time, but always kept up a brave face for her two kids, ages 11 and 8. She did a good job hiding what she must have felt in order to be the mom and wife she wanted to be. Before she was admitted to the hospital for what would be her last days, she left a handwritten note on the refrigerator door: [through tears and with a broken voice] "Always meet them more than halfway." That's it. That's how my sister lived her life. That's what she wanted her family to do.*
>
> *And that's what I encourage all of you to do this year with everyone you deal with: fellow teachers, students, parents, administrators . . . everyone. Always meet them more than halfway. You have my promise that that is how I will strive to do my job as your superintendent. [pause] Thank you for all you do. Have a great year.*

What do you think of this talk?

1. Is this a message you would want to hear on opening day? Why or why not?
2. How would you have responded—positively or negatively?
3. How do you think most of the attendees responded?

Plan a welcoming talk for the new school year.

1. List all thoughts that might be going through the minds of the listeners.
2. What do you want the #1 takeaway from your talk to be?

3. What comments would you like to hear after your talk?
4. What content would be likely to lead to you receiving those comments?

Exercise 2

Look back at the case study on pages 38–39 and critique Suzanne's talk at the 4th grade show.

1. What message do you think parents attending the show expected to hear?
2. Did Suzanne's content fit the occasion?
3. What should have been in Suzanne's Must Include category?
4. What should have been in Suzanne's Don't Include category?

Exercise 3

You have two meetings scheduled to talk with two teachers who have each received a parent complaint about the same issue: the parents feel the teachers are not doing enough to stop bullying in class. Because you read Chapter 1, before you speak, you think about your audience and write down what you know about each teacher:

Jennifer: A 15-year veteran, teaches 8th grade, moody (sometimes warm and approachable, sometimes ice cold), follows procedures to the letter, runs a tight ship, can rub people the wrong way, the building rep for the teachers' association, an avid outdoorswoman

Marty: First-year teacher, teaches 7th grade, happy-go-lucky, great sense of humor, takes an unstructured approach (lesson plans are usually just suggestions in his mind), classroom is often loud, big football fan, has expressed interest in moving into administration one day

You need to make the same main point in your message to both these teachers.

1. How will the message you design for Jennifer differ from the message you design for Marty?
2. How will you establish connections with each of these teachers?
3. What responses will you prepare for?
4. What positives will you offer each?

3

What You Shouldn't Say

Even if you create a talk that includes all the right elements, that talk can be torpedoed by one inaccurate or unwise comment or even a comment that is misinterpreted.

There are certainly times in my life where I wished I could go back and unsay something. Often it was a spur-of-the-moment comment; a little "think before you speak" would have helped. Occasionally, a planned-out talk creates problems too. And although no one *intends* to say the wrong thing, this chapter discusses some of what is in the Don't Include category to help remind you of what *not* to say before you speak. Analyzing the audience will help, of course, but I want to provide some high-level and widely applicable advice.

Avoid "Public Speaking Language"

Many speakers assume that because speeches tend to be associated with big occasions, big words and formal language are required. Quite the opposite. More often than not, formal language and fancy vocabulary words are inappropriate and should be avoided.

Who is in your audience, and what level of formality is appropriate to them? That's the level of formality you need for your spoken message. What is the simplest way to say what you want to say? Those are the words you need.

As I was writing this book, I kept noticing how often I was hearing speakers swap in the word *utilize* for the word *use*. A sports announcer told me that Miguel Cabrera *utilizes* a bigger bat than most players. A newscaster mentioned that rescuers *utilized* a rope ladder to save a trapped animal. An educator talked about *utilizing* project-based learning in their school. Is the idea that bigger words convey importance and make you sound more intelligent? They don't. You don't have to utilize words that are overutilized in an attempt to sound official or authoritative or smart. Use the simplest language possible and use words that are comfortable for your listeners.

Here's a look at some phrasing I hear all the time in education-related talks, along with alternate phrasing that I think sounds more natural and is more likely to help you connect with your audience.

Stilted and Pretentious: Avoid	**More Natural and Relatable: Try Instead**
Tony indicated to me	Tony said
At this point in time, we should...	Now, we should...
With regard to the previous comment, I think...	I think...
Could you inform us as to whether...	Tell us whether...
We have the pleasure to announce...	I'm happy to say...
If you need assistance...	If you need help...
It is believed that this program...	We believe this program...
We achieved positive results utilizing...	We got good results using...
The desired learning outcomes include...	Students should learn...

Avoid Ed-Speak

Rigor. Grit. Unpack. Learning loss. Differentiation. All of these made an *Education Week* Top 10 list of words educators never wanted to hear again (Hardison, 2022). You probably have your own least favorite trendy terms to add to this list. My point is, even listeners who understand education jargon are tired of it.

That doesn't mean it is a bad idea to foster grit. Perseverance is certainly worth developing, and tenacity is useful when trying to solve tough problems. I support encouraging students to remain determined even when they face setbacks. Did you notice that I used three words that mean the same thing as *grit,* because *grit* now grates? Notice when you use specialized or clichéd education terms. If you rely on them all the time, break the habit.

While those in education are tired of hearing ed-speak, those outside education are flat-out mystified by the terms we tend to use. I mean, lots of educators agree that using portfolios to assess higher-order thinking is a noble goal. We know that implementing scaffolding in Tier 1 language arts instruction might involve applying research-based reading strategies, including whole language, embedded phonics, and decoding. And I believe that graphic organizers are effective supports for activating background knowledge. Now step back and reread those last three sentences with new eyes. Is there any question that educators speak in code? Although ed-speak is a language that is largely unknown to parents, I hear administrators speaking it all the time at new student orientations, PTCO meetings, Back-to-School Nights, and more.

Jargon can be a shortcut in certain circumstances, but it risks, in Theresa Stager's words, making the listeners "feel 'left out.' It makes them feel behind right off the bat, and that isn't a great way to have your audiences feel at the beginning of your presentation." Jargon may do nothing but confuse and irritate an audience composed of parents, community members, and local business owners who don't know what those words mean.

Similarly, be careful with education-related abbreviations and acronyms—the strings of PLC, MTSS, SEL, EOY, AMI, DEI, RTI, and so forth—what Steven Weber and others refer to as "alphabet soup." It's true that if your school offers project-based learning, it can be difficult to avoid mentioning PBL. If there is a situation where an acronym is unavoidable or particularly useful, define it first and provide an example. Jessica Holloway provides this useful reminder:

> Many in the field of education do not understand all the jargon and abbreviations out there. It is unfair to think noneducators will catch on or figure it out in context. Clear is kind, so kindly and clearly explain a specialized term before using it in your message.

Every field of expertise has its own language. Good communicators recognize that and are quick to offer translations for those who are not experts in the field.

Avoid Wordiness

Imagine yourself in the audience at a school board meeting. Speakers have signed up to comment about the closing of two neighborhood elementary schools, which will mean transferring the students to schools farther from home. The assistant superintendent opens the meeting like this:

> *Let me make some brief comments to begin. I know there are lots of people who have signed up to speak tonight, so I will keep my remarks short. The decision was not an easy one. We know neighborhood schools are important. I want to give a little explanation of the rationale behind the decision. In the interest of time, I won't go through all of the enrollment and budget numbers but will give a quick overview of the fiscal situation. I think that will be a useful starting point for understanding. So, if you will bear with me for a little bit, I'll give you a quick look at the numbers behind the decision. Willow Creek enrollment has dropped from 617 in 2016 to 380 this year; Stenson enrollment fell from 577 to 347 in the same timeframe. . . .*

Any time someone says they will be brief, they have already failed to be as brief as they could have been. Extra words are what I call *verbal glut*. They add no value. I think many of the assistant superintendent's words qualify as verbal glut and could easily be cut:

> ~~Let me make some brief comments to begin. I know there are lots of people who have signed up to speak tonight so I will keep my remarks short.~~ *The decision was not an easy one. We know neighborhood schools are important. I want to give a little explanation of the rationale behind the decision.* ~~In the interest of time, I won't go through all of the enrollment and budget numbers but will give a quick overview of the fiscal situation. I think that will be a useful starting point for understanding. So, if you will bear with me for little bit, I'll give you a quick look at the numbers behind the decision.~~ *Willow Creek enrollment has dropped from 617 in 2016 to 380 this year; Stenson enrollment fell from 577 to 347 in the same timeframe....*

I just cut those remarks from 140 words to 50 words. What remains has more impact because the essential information stands out. Listeners don't have to sift through excess verbiage to find the valuable parts.

There are other types of verbal glut, including stories that don't contribute to the speaker's objective, unnecessary details that distract from the intended message, and digressions that derail the audience's attention from what's important to understand. For example:

> *I'm trying to remember who was originally on that curriculum committee. I think Terry was before he took the position at ESC and maybe Nikki. No, come to think of it, not Nikki because she was still working with assessment. Anyhow, the current committee....*

Be ruthless in cutting this type of content.

For more important talks, always write a script. True, you won't read from it at speaking time, but preparing will help to ensure that you have included all the ideas you intend as well as all the "things you should say" covered in Chapter 2, and it will let you see where glut may be creeping in. No one has time to script everything they say, though, so you may discover excess verbiage after the fact. If you are like I am, you play back talks in your mind: "I wish I had said . . . . I think I got a good reaction when I said . . . ." As you evaluate your talks, add a "glut check" to your analysis: "Didn't I already cover that topic with everyone on the committee? Drat. That was unnecessary." Over time, you'll get better at producing focused speech.

Case Study

After a faculty breakfast in the cafeteria and two hours of work in their respective classrooms, teachers reported for grade-level meetings on the first day back, one week before students were scheduled to report for the new school year.

The 16 teachers on the 8th grade team were anxious to meet their administrator, a new assistant principal whose hiring was announced only a few days earlier. They knew little about her. After about a 10-minute wait, a woman they had never seen before walked into the room. Here's what she said:

Hello, I'm Lydia. What I'd like to do at every meeting is share a strategy-focused article for you to read and implement. The article I'm handing out now is about praise. Most of you are praising students incorrectly. Read this article and be prepared to discuss it at our next meeting. I'll share a new article at every meeting this year.

And with that, Lydia walked out. There was no "I'm looking forward to getting to know you." There were no questions and no asking teachers to share their names, subject taught, or tenure at the school. There were no pleasantries of any sort. (The article discussed the difference between "Wow, you're really smart"— a fixed trait—and "Wow, you are working really hard on this"— a growth-mindset trait.)

Avoid Reprimands and Threats

Remember the story I shared about the head of school who opened the year with a reminder to flush the toilet? A *remarkably* inappropriate comment for the situation, right? There everybody was, on their first day back on campus after more than a year of COVID remote learning, and the welcome they got was toilet-related finger wagging? Special situation aside, a group conversation is never the place for reprimands. As the adage goes, *praise in public, reprimand in private.*

As a leader, sometimes it is your job to crack the whip and get results. You have a mission, and tolerating dissent will just slow you down. Except, of course, that is not how life works. A sure way to lose those you are supposed to lead toward success is to threaten them along the way.

Scott Petrie is a high school teacher in Granada Hills, California. He told me a story about a principal who came to the year's first staff meeting with a little red wagon. I'll talk more about the wagon in Chapter 4, but it's a metaphor you see employed from time to time in workplace speeches, generally to communicate that sometimes, making progress requires pulling others along, sometimes it requires pushing from the back, and sometimes it means just being along for the ride. Scott's principal took the metaphor further—too far. This is how Scott describes it:

> Somewhere, the wagon metaphor kind of took a turn for the sinister. The principal talked about how "some people will help me pull, some people will help me push, and other people will take their hammers and try to break the wheels off. If you're one of those people, look out! I'm coming for you!"
>
> Educators don't respond well to threats, and I think this principal got off on a bad foot. I don't think his leadership was ever as collaborative and positive as he would have liked. There was a chill in the atmosphere, and from that point on, teachers were leery of this guy. [The school] developed a culture of punishment. [For] math teachers who had a high number of failure rates, instead of coaching and lifting these teachers up it was, "I'm going to punish you. I'm going to write you up. I'm going to drive you out of my school." It made the relationship needlessly

adversarial. This chill made a lot of teachers very wary of participating in leadership committees that tried to advance professional development or tried to advance curriculum. People just stopped participating, and our school is still struggling to overcome this.

Remember the unavoidable Us versus Them attitude between leaders and those being led. Before you speak, ask yourself what words will widen the gap and which words will diminish or help to bridge it.

Avoid Careless Speech That Sends Unintended Messages

It is common for people to read between the lines. We get an email, and we add meaning to it—making guesses about what the sender is really thinking ("She seems upset") or feeling ("He seems really overwhelmed right now"). We also listen between the lines when people speak to us.

Meghan Everette shares this example:

> I had a principal once who was not good with interpersonal relationships. He stepped in communication messes all the time. An example is when he wanted me to move from 1st to 3rd grade and said, "I'm moving you to 3rd grade next year; I'm starting to believe you are kind of smart." The implications of that are pretty terrible. *You didn't think I was smart when you hired me? You think that the rest of my team isn't smart enough to teach 3rd grade, but I am, so I'm the one that moves?* There are so many instances of these remarks from him.

Listening between the lines, Meghan heard some "pretty terrible" things. On top of what she pointed out, I also "heard" the principal imply that smart people don't teach 1st grade—an offense to 1st grade teachers everywhere. But Meghan's principal no doubt thought he was giving her a compliment and was oblivious to the implied insults. The defense that he didn't mean it "like that" doesn't fix the problem; Meghan heard it like that, and now we have too.

Recall my principal who boasted about being "an ulcer carrier." I read between the lines to come up with my idea of what kind of leader she was. Another principal I knew was fond of saying, "I want what's best for students" every time teachers tried to give input on one of her directives. The between-the-lines message? *"You* don't know what is best for students" or perhaps even worse, "You don't *care* what's best for students." I don't know if she intended for us to get those hidden messages or if she was simply unaware of how the phrase sounded to us.

To complicate things further, we are living in an era in which everyone seems to be on high alert when it comes to messages and messaging—quick to take offense and point out errors. A slight comment can cause a major blow-up, and people seem to delight in playing "Gotcha!" All the more reason to think very seriously about how listeners might interpret or misinterpret your words before you open your mouth.

Might comments you intended as praise carry unintended insults, like those Meghan heard? Do you sometimes choose words that have possible double meanings? ("She was really a wicked teacher!") Are some of your constructions ambiguous and open to misinterpretation? ("The teacher was reprimanding the student, and she hit her." Was it the teacher who hit the student, or the student who hit the teacher?) Be very careful in thinking about how your audience might get a message that is different from what you intend.

Avoid Information Better Shared in Other Formats

"Let me tell you all about—no, wait. Just read it yourself."

These lines should be spoken far more than they are. Lots of information that is shared orally is often better shared in written form. Here's an example. At my schools, teachers always got our test score reports from the spring state assessments in the fall. Every year, a faculty meeting was used to share all the data. Grade by grade, subject by subject, all the results were projected on a screen and read aloud. They weren't discussed or unpacked; they were just read—shared for the very first time. It was quite time-consuming... and it was completely unnecessary in an era when our leaders could have just emailed a link for us to click through and read at our convenience.

Keith Young believes that the Don't Include category includes "routine information and updates to educational materials, data and reports, and meeting minutes and action items." He argues that the following topics make more sense to cover in written communication that is shared digitally:

- Information about upcoming events, deadlines, policy changes, and meetings
- Teachers' guides, lesson plans, and professional development resources
- Student performance data, progress reports, and attendance records
- Post-meeting summaries and action items, along with who's responsible for them

By all means, comment on these topics in meetings to share the big picture, highlight progress and excellence, or point out spots where you're falling short. Hold in-person discussions of necessary responses. But communicate the detailed information in a form that your staff can examine closely, reference, and return to. Is there a risk that some teachers won't study the data in your email or post on your school's communication platform? Sure, but they're likely to be the same teachers who would not have paid attention or taken notes if the data were read to them.

Michael Pinto likes the idea of using a site such as Canva to create "one-pagers"—easily shareable graphics covering all the key information. As he says,

> I can send information in this form again and again through different formats, like Instagram or Facebook or email. I can save it to my phone, and I can be very streamlined.

Michael uses one-page graphics to communicate with staff and parents, freeing up meeting time. He also shares general information:

> I share an email each morning called "Morning Message" with my staff and several others who have asked to receive it. It's a quote or a laugh or something I write myself. It usually has meaning for our mission

of instruction or staff climate or humanity. It's my slow weathering of thought that helps to shape a school culture. I've done this for two decades spanning two schools.

He could have made a morning announcement over the school's PA system but decided to put it in writing instead. A caveat: when you have a more expansive communication space like a newsletter, it can be tempting to dump too much information at once. Steven Weber has made this mistake:

> As a principal, I shared a weekly newsletter with staff. It outlined district updates and curriculum resources, shared YouTube videos, and provided school announcements. At the time, I felt like I was curating resources and saving teachers and staff time from searching the internet, but now I see that I was probably overcommunicating. A bi-weekly newsletter would have provided teachers and staff with more time to read and implement suggestions. Finally, I should have met with a group of teachers and staff and asked them how the newsletter was received. Feedback from focus groups could have helped me revise the product in order to improve the newsletter.

These comments remind us again how important audience analysis is. Even well-intentioned communication can fail to serve an audience if it does not align with their needs.

Audience Analysis Redux

All the Don't Include categories I've covered to this point are universal. Always avoid public-speaking language, always cut verbal glut, always avoid threats, and so on. Sometimes, though, there is more nuance involved. Words that can turn off or alienate some audiences will resonate strongly with others and get them on your side. An inside joke that establishes rapport will be obscure to and exclusionary to others.

This is why you must do your homework before you speak to individuals too. Learn the senses of humor you're dealing with. Who enjoys trash talking? Who can you let your hair down with? While professionalism is necessary, the most buttoned-up form of professionalism is not always what is called for or what will work best, and walking on eggshells can be exhausting. I am a person who likes kidding around. It's good for my mental health. So, I take the time to identify colleagues who share this mindset, and we all benefit:

Kelly: Well, *that* parent conversation went well!
Me: I know, right? You really messed that one up.
Kelly: As if you would have done better!
Me: I couldn't have done worse.
Kelly: Whatever! Anyway, that was a tough one.
Me: It's a shame there are people like that.

Here's an exchange that could be interpreted as me first insulting my colleague Kelly and then moving on to judge a parent. But I know that I can be my joking self with Kelly and can say things to her I should not and would not say to everyone or in front of others. Take the time to find your safe spaces.

The Simple Takeaway

Good speakers know what *not to say* as well as what *to say*. Many problems that educational leaders encounter can be avoided if they carefully think about the Don't Include category as they craft their messages. Whether avoiding jargon, glut, clichés, or "fancy" language or being aware of unintended messages, knowing what to leave out of the talk can be as important as what to put into a talk.

Application Exercises

Exercise 1

Look back at the case study about Lydia's first meeting with the 8th grade team.

1. What did Lydia say that she should not have said?
2. What were the unintended messages the 8th grade staff got?

3. How would you have begun that meeting?
4. How would you have introduced the article?

Exercise 2

A 2nd grade teacher is often heard being sarcastic with students:

> *Student:* What page are we on?
> *Teacher:* Well, if you had your brain turned on today, you'd know. Page 45.
>
> *Student:* Is the answer 14?
> *Teacher:* Why are you *asking* me? You're supposed to know.

Aside from this bad habit, she is a good teacher, and you want to keep a positive relationship with her—a walking-on-eggshells conversation is needed. Craft the message you will give to her, taking the following steps:

1. Invent a profile of the teacher and give her some personality so you can do an audience analysis.
2. Based on your profile, make two lists: *Must Include* and *Don't Include*. Having the lists to look at will keep you from inadvertently saying something that you are thinking but that won't be productive.
3. Find someone to role-play with you and test out your talk.

4

How to Present Your Message

Typically, tradition dictates the style of a presentation.

For example, when I first began speaking in front of groups, I used a pad of chart paper on a big easel. Everyone did. Now people speaking at faculty meetings and giving conference presentations use presentation software—overwhelmingly PowerPoint. Speakers at PTCO meetings use the microphone at the podium. Webinars and online meetings use platforms like Zoom.

You are probably visualizing various kinds of educational talks and presentations right now. Add detail to that visualization for a minute. Imagine how big the room is and how it is set up. See where the speaker will stand—or the pathways the speaker will walk throughout the room. Think about what the slides will look like, what the Zoom thumbnail will be. You know how these things go. You know what normal is.

The problem is that *normal is boring.* True, no one will complain if you do what has always been done, but no one will be particularly impressed, either. The challenge I want to lay out is for you to start looking at the talks and presentations you give—big ones and small ones, formal ones and informal ones—and see them with new eyes. Reimagine what's possible. Your audience will thank you for it.

Advice for Presenting in Person

I'm guessing that most of your talks are given in person. In fact, I'd wager that in-person talks are so common that you don't think too much about what you might do to present yourself in the best possible light. Meeting with a teacher or a parent; running a faculty meeting or a PLC; leading professional development—been there, done that, right? You've got that handled. But let me suggest that in spite of your experience and in spite of how everyone else does it, you can be more engaging and effective with some purposeful forethought and some changed behaviors. Let me show you how.

Be present and accessible

For most staff, points of contact with leaders are comparatively rare. Consider that teachers do not generally approach the head of school about everyday issues, and they may hear the superintendent speak in person once a year, if that. So, for leaders, being present in small moments with staff members can enhance your ability to communicate across the board. Meghan Everette puts it this way:

> When administrators or coaches regularly visit classrooms and are visible in the school, it lessens the anxiety around pop-ins, but also leads to better understanding of what is happening in the school as a whole. That authentic knowledge and understanding helps build trust as well. I worked in a school where members of the administration walked around daily and popped into my room, even briefly, once a week (if not more). I felt they knew me, my kids, my style, and what was really happening throughout the building. By contrast, teachers I worked with in coaching felt anxious and on guard when administration came around because they were seen so infrequently, it felt like any observation would be a judgment. They didn't think administrators had a fair reference for what was typical.

Good leaders are present every day. Being accessible does two things: it gives you more opportunities to share your messages and your philosophy, and it makes connections that will help your big talks be received better. Choose to present often in low-stakes situations to better set up your presentations in high-stakes situations.

Take the time to understand the physical setup

For many in-person presentations, the location dictates how you should present—at least to some extent.

Some locations are familiar. Will you be in your school's auditorium, standing on a stage, at a lectern, with a fixed microphone? Will you be in a noisy hallway, the school cafeteria during lunch, standing in a classroom in front of parents squeezed into their grade school children's small desks?

Other talks will be in unfamiliar places. If you'll be giving a big presentation in a space you don't know well, make sure to learn a little bit about the location's logistics in advance. Will there be a podium? Will there be a fixed microphone? Which side of the podium will the screen be on? How will your audience be seated—theater-style, in front-facing rows with an easy eyeline to you and your slides, or at round tables so that some will need to turn to see you? Will you be projecting slides on a screen in a conference room? You need to know where the projector will be, where your computer will be, and where the sound controls are. It may be important to know where the thermostat is. No matter where you present, there should be no surprises, and you should be able to foresee how the logistics will affect your talk.

Because you know that all talks require audience analysis, consider what your presentation will look like, feel like, and sound like to them, from *their* point of view. If you will be speaking into a microphone, where in the room are the speakers located? Will everyone be able to see you easily? How comfortable are the chairs? What level of lighting will there be? Will there be auditory distractions from outside—noises from the next room or from the street? Will there be wi-fi? Will everyone have a laptop or phone handy, meaning you'll need to counter audience members' temptation to scroll, text, or do other work?

I have presented in large rooms with great acoustics that allowed me to be microphone free as I moved around the space. I've talked in small rooms with lots of noises from adjacent rooms and hallways that forced me to use a microphone and be tethered to a podium. I've altered break schedules because attendees were in uncomfortable plastic chairs and needed to move. I've changed activities because listeners in rows can't easily do what listeners at round tables can do. Think about how it would feel and look to be in your audience, imagine their perspective, and adjust how you present based on these variables.

Choose a message-enhancing setting when that is an option

Outside of a larger presentation, there is often a choice about the location and logistics. Instead of "Where do you have to present, and what will that mean?" the question becomes "Where do you *want* to present, and how will that affect your message?" Think of your purpose. Make decisions purposefully.

Here are some examples:

- Where do you want to be when you need to reprimand a teacher for a poor choice? Yes, of course you will opt for a private setting for this kind of talk, but do you want to be seated on one side of a desk, talking to the teacher who is seated on the other side? That choice would convey a sense of formality, add gravitas, and underscore your power. Is that the choice you want to make? Why or why not?
- What about giving a teacher feedback after an observation? Having this talk in the teacher's classroom while you are sitting in a student chair is less adversarial and may be the way to go.
- Where should the 8th grade administrator ask the 8th grade teachers to gather for their weekly meetings? Always in Randy's room, which is comfortable and has good light at the scheduled meeting time? Or should the location rotate so that teachers can get a sense of one another's style and get an equal chance to "host"?

- Does every faculty meeting need to be in the school library, and must every meeting involve a PowerPoint presentation? What are the potential alternatives? Maybe "data dump" informational meetings should be held in one place (with a screen at the front and seats in rows) and working meetings with discussion held somewhere with tables—a setting more conducive to collaboration? And is there a place where everyone could gather for quick stand-up meetings? Ten minutes might be all the time needed for a couple of announcements that you'd like to make in person: "Erika is our teacher of the year!" and "Our DECA team advisor has some news to share."

Choose a message-enhancing presentation style

Will you be giving an information-dense lecture or an inspiration-rich pep talk? Will you be using slides? Will you be guiding a discussion? Leading a brainstorming session? Participating in a Q&A? Interviewing panelists and spotlighting their individual messages?

There are choices, and you can make them! Just because every professional development leader and conference speaker you have seen in the past 20 years used PowerPoint slides doesn't mean all such talks demand PowerPoint. And even if you use PowerPoint, there are different ways to structure the presentation, as Jessica Holloway shares:

> I had an opportunity to present an Ignite Session at ASCD's 2022 Annual Conference with a group of emerging leaders. I had never presented in this style before and was curious how it would go.
>
> Ignite presentations are 20 slides long, with 15 seconds allotted for each slide, making for a total of 5 minutes on stage. Knowing this, I had to be clear and concise with my words and images to articulate a cohesive message. There is no reading off the screen. It's set up so that the slides will advance automatically at 15-second intervals, which creates a sense of urgency. I planned and rehearsed. I found the Ignite Session (combined presentations into a full 60-minute session) to be a tremendous growth experience as a speaker.

The times where you're planning your normal, everyday educational messages are great opportunities to think outside the box and

How to Present Your Message

experiment. A 10-minute stand-up meeting in the upper commons again? No, it's a beautiful day, so let's meet on the blacktop outside the cafeteria. A post-observation conference in the teacher's classroom? No, we've been in that room for an hour already; how about a walk-and-talk? Variety in presentation style is refreshing and can make even lower-stakes talks like these more memorable and effective. Just because the last superintendent came to the faculty meeting, spoke for 15 minutes, and answered teacher questions for 15 minutes doesn't mean that you must follow that model.

Some situations deserve a bit more attention, and how you choose to present may be critical. For instance, how should you present potentially sensitive or "cringe-y" content? The latter is Scott Petrie's term. He told me how he and the other 120 teachers at his school were asked to report to the cafeteria for a presentation on an unnamed topic. So they trooped in, sat down at random, and were told the topic would be grooming—not the kind of grooming pets get or *grooming* in the sense of apprenticing before taking on a new job role but grooming in the sense of establishing an emotional connection with a child in the hope of starting a sexual relationship. The principal cued up a training video showing a female teacher and her female student in a series of conversations. Periodically, the principal paused the movie, pointed at talking-point prompts, and asked staff members to discuss these with others at their table. Massive awkwardness ensued. Teachers weren't necessarily seated with trusted friends or even in departmental groups. Was this an ideal setup for open discussion about very uncomfortable content?

Contrast this with the approach counselor Gabrielle Price takes. When she leads the mandated reporting talk or meetings about boundaries or other sensitive or uncomfortable topics, she chooses her presentation mode carefully:

> First of all, we let people know the day before that the conversation is coming. Second, we kind of prepare the group in person once we're there: if you need to step out, if you need to rearrange your seat, if you need to participate at the level you're able to . . . we let people find their own comfort level. We do have interactive parts, but it is rarely a discussion.

We may show a case study of teachers texting with students and have people as a group rate it red, green, or yellow—is this terrible, is this OK, or is this something in between—because sharing out as a group is a little easier.

Note that Gabrielle understands the audience and adapts to *their* needs. She also chooses a style of interaction that is less threatening for participants. In both Scott's and Gabrielle's examples, key content was presented by video. That is a legitimate presentation choice and generally a safe way to approach sensitive topics.

Even those who give talks for very large audiences have choices of how to present. I have spoken at many conferences and attended even more. I'm always paying attention to speakers' choices, and I have seen, for example, that speakers given the same size room with the same setup and the same hour-long block will handle these circumstances very differently.

Within the same year, I attended four different conferences—each with a keynote session in which the advertised speaker appeared before the entire group of conference attendees for 60 minutes. Author Seth Godin talked for that entire hour, accompanied by a fast-paced slide show. Former president Barack Obama sat in a chair and answered questions posed by a moderator seated opposite him. Educator Gerry Brooks used props, video clips, and slides. And Oprah Winfrey made a few remarks and then fielded questions from the audience. In other words, a keynote structure is not set—the speakers chose the style. Do you want to present on stage at the front of the room? While walking around the room? Do you want to open up the floor for questions? Use visual aids? Think about the best style of presentation to suit your purpose.

Advice for Using Visual Aids

Speaking of visual aids....

Once I was asked to speak at a large gathering of teachers and parents at California State University at San Marcos. The wrinkle? The talk was outdoors. Typically, when I speak, I highlight my message using

PowerPoint slides on a screen. But on this sunny morning, outside and in front of 1,500 people, there was no projector-and-screen combination that would work. So I went without my trusted visual aids and . . . the presentation was still a success. My message still worked, all by itself. The experience led me to rethink visual aids in general and my use of them specifically. I realized that I'd let myself be boxed in by "my normal." Maybe you're in the same situation.

Rethink your standard approach

When it comes to using visual aids in your presentation, start by asking what you want visual aids to do. This question may never have occurred to you; I know there was a long time before it occurred to me. I had learned through the experience of attending conferences and workshops how these presentations were "supposed to go," and I just followed the models I had seen. I had internalized that staff developers, consultants, instructional coaches, principals, conference speakers—everyone, essentially—used slides during their presentations and made a slide for each critical point. But there's so much thought that can and should go into these decisions when you stop doing what you've always done and consider what you might do instead. For example, do you want to use a visual aid to

- Reinforce a concept?
- Leave a memorable impression?
- Hype the audience up?
- Introduce a topic?
- Clarify an idea?
- Be printed and put into a binder no one will ever look at again?
- Redundantly reiterate what you just said?
- Give the audience something to read while you talk?
- Remind you what you are supposed to say?

Yes, while the last four items on this list are poor reasons to make visual aids, many are made for exactly those reasons. However, focusing on the first five questions is a good way to rethink your standard approach and experiment with more purposeful, meaningful, and unique visual aids.

Eliminate distracting elements

As a basic rule, all visual aids distract somewhat from your words. If listeners are looking at a visual, they are not looking at you or giving your words their undivided attention.

For those fearful of public speaking, having listeners distracted by visual aids might sound appealing, but that's not a good reason for visual aids. As a leader, you always want the focus to be on you and your message. Michael Pinto shared that when he was a young administrator, he prepared transparencies for a presentation he was set to give in front of his school and his boss. (Younger readers will have to look up "overhead projector" and "transparencies.") In his words,

> A large initiative our school undertook was adopting standards-based report cards. I was prepared. I had my transparencies all together. I gave the presentation, and it was a success. But I had used about 50 transparencies on an overhead projector. When I finished, the superintendent looked at me and said, "Great job. Next time, PowerPoint." Of course, he was right. I had taken away from the presentation by my constant shuffling of overhead transparencies. The visuals should add to, not detract from, your message.

How often have you lost contact with a speaker because you were distracted by something the presenter was showing you? Even if Michael had followed the superintendent's advice and used PowerPoint, the distraction problem could remain. Sure, shuffling sheets of plastic is very distracting, but even if smoothly handled, people looking at the screen are not looking at the speaker. You don't want anyone reading from the screen or analyzing your artwork when you are making a point.

So: should you always have visual aids? No. But you should always make purposeful decisions about how to present each part of a talk. "I need something here for clarification, but for the next section, I want total focus on me, so I'll black out the projector. I'll add a reinforcement slide after that"—that's the thought process that will help make your presentations more engaging and effective.

Consider props

Let's assume that you've decided that your talk would benefit from some visual enhancement. The default is PowerPoint or some alternative slide-creating program. What if you used props instead?

Short for "property" in the language of stage and film, props are objects that are placed on a set to provide a context for the scene. If an actor walks in wearing a lab coat and holding a beaker, before a word is said, we the audience are thinking "scientist." Remember Scott Petrie's principal with the red wagon? A brilliant prop—and something Scott remembers years later. (Yes, the metaphor took a turn for the worse, but the wagon concept was good.) Gerry Brooks often goes on stage with a little bag containing a few props. I won't mention all of them, but— spoiler alert!—I will tell you that at one point, he reaches into the bag and pulls out a baby pacifier. You're intrigued, right? Why a pacifier? I won't tell Gerry's story, but I will tell you that everyone who hears him tell that story remembers the pacifier and what it stands for.

Is there an item that absolutely represents a point you are trying to make? A well-chosen prop can make a great and lasting impression.

A Closer Look at Better Slide Use

Slide presentations are not the only option for visual aids, but because they are the default—in education and beyond—it's worth focusing on them specifically and providing some illustration.

We have a hard time imagining presenting without PowerPoint or one of its slide-making competitors. That's fine! Slides are great... or they *can* be great, with a little more attention. Let me share ideas for those who are committed to using a slide deck and want to use slides well.

I'm sure I'm not the only one who has received a presentation handout that was a picture of every slide accompanied by blank lines for notes. There was a time when this was the standard, and I think the idea was that attendees could take notes about the presenter's remarks and revisit the presentation later. The enormous amount of paper needed to print a hundred slides for 50 attendees basically ended that practice, but it would have ended sooner if clearer thinking had prevailed. Because no one *ever* looked at the handout later.

Ugly slides aren't worth saving (and ugly is normal, as we'll discuss in a minute), but it took environmental and cost concerns to change the behavior. The changes in slide design I'm proposing won't help the environment and won't save money. But they will dramatically improve your audience's experience by reinforcing your concepts, being memorable, stimulating listener interest, and clarifying your ideas—and these are all the best reasons for using visuals in the first place.

Rule 1: Remember your purpose

Many presenters spend enormous amounts of time creating a slide deck as if the deck is the most important piece of a presentation. It isn't. The speaker and the message are. We create slide decks to help accomplish our purpose, not to stand in for us. A slide is an *aid,* a helper.

Case Study

At a national conference for a major educational organization, an author and consultant presented on the topic "Creating Great Leadership Teams." Because the presenter was well known, he spoke in one of the biggest rooms in the convention center.

He started the talk by announcing there were three things necessary to set the groundwork for a great team: "First, you need to agree on one vision. This can take some time and effort." After spending a few minutes explaining the concept, he walked to a table behind the podium, drew on his tablet, and projected something that looked like this onto the screen:

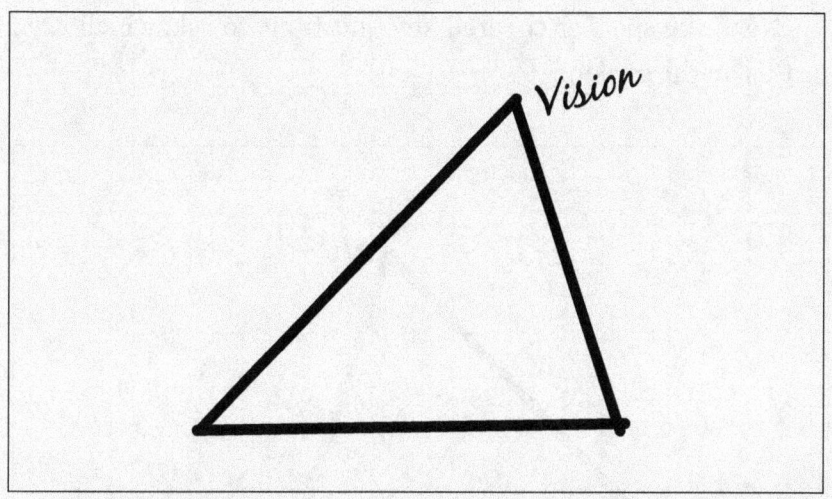

The talk continued from there, following the same pattern. The speaker would introduce a key term, explain its importance, and pause to go back to the tablet and add the term to the graphic on the screen. First, he added two additional groundwork elements (purpose, goals), then he described the three attributes that team members must have (commitment, integrity, openness to change). After 20 minutes or so, this is what we in the audience were looking at.

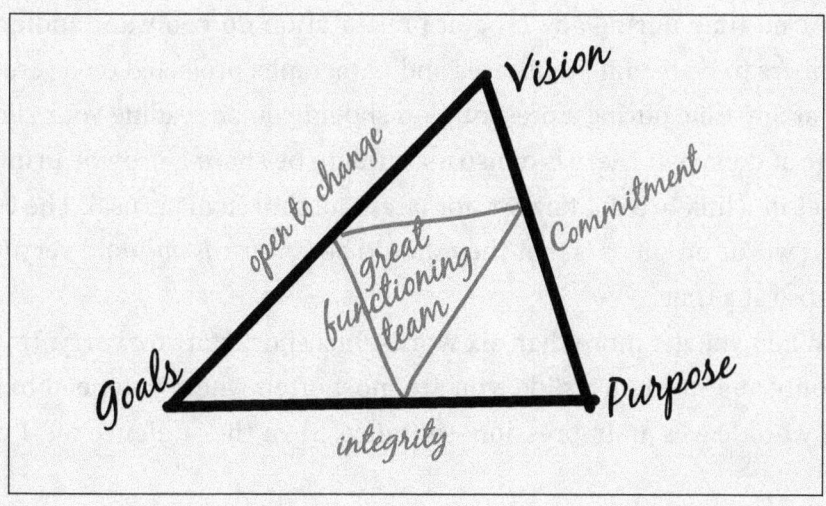

Next, the speaker covered key questions to ask, which gave us this on the screen:

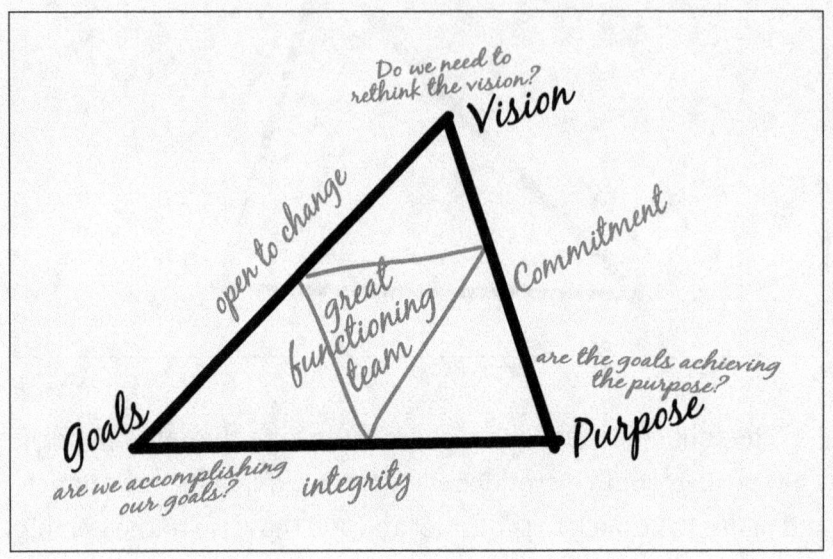

Rule 2: Never use complete sentences

"Read along silently as I read the words aloud." This is classic teacher language, and it's a horrible presenter strategy.

At no time during any type of presentation do you want audience members to be reading sentences and paragraphs projected on a screen. Nor at any time during a presentation should you be reading your slides *to* the audience. If there is dense material to be shared, provide printed copies or a link to a digital copy for later and thorough perusal. The rule about words on slides is that they should be *key words only* and very few of those at a time.

When you get more than six words on a slide, start to worry. If you get only one word on a slide, you are most often where you need to be. One word leaves an impression; sentences turn the audience off. I can hear you asking, *But one word—how can that be enough?* It's not enough on its own, but that is why you're there. Your job, as the presenter, is to explain. Tell listeners why that word is important. This approach is more likely to keep the audience's attention and leave an impression.

Rule 3: Never use your slides as a crutch

Earlier in this chapter, we heard Jessica Holloway talk about the Ignite presentation format: a total of 20 slides that automatically advance every 15 seconds. This format is not foolproof, however. Jessica also told me of a presenter whose approach was to read each slide—which only took five seconds—and then stand silently for 10 seconds waiting for the slide to advance. Problem 1: the presenter sort of missed the point about having 15 seconds to work with. Problem 2: the presenter was slide bound. He had the slide to read and nothing else planned to say.

Now, if you follow Rule 2 and avoid slides with complete sentences, Problem 2 will be less of a factor. But there is still a risk that a less prepared, less practiced speaker will use slides as a reminder: "Oh yeah, I also want to say ____." The purpose of slides is to aid the audience, not help the speaker. Proper practice means you will know what you are going to say, right? But if the content is hard to memorize (e.g., a long quote from an expert or some detailed data) or if you think nervousness might lead to forgetfulness, keep a separate set of notes to glance at. We'll talk in the next section about performance skills, but watching someone read is far less engaging than listening to a good speaker.

Rule 4: Think of the big picture

When I taught elementary school, I occasionally assigned presentations with a visual aid requirement. Sometimes I suspected that Dad went to the store the night before the presentation to buy a piece of poster board so the student could scribble something on it. Often, students would start their talks by commenting, "I know you can't see this from the back of the room, but . . . ." When they did, I would gently comment that the *point* of a visual aid is to be helpful—and visible—to all audience members. Sadly, there are many adults who could have benefitted from that insight.

Most presenters design their presentation slides on the computer screen right in front of them. The slides look OK from a foot away. But few presenters imagine how slides will look to all audience members on presentation day. A lot of work might go into making a detailed slide, but to anyone not sitting at the forward-most table, it will be unreadable.

When it comes to slide design, always begin with the big picture. That means asking, "Will this slide work for everyone in attendance?" Be inclusive. Will those with less than perfect vision be able to access the slide's information? Will all attendees be able to read a red word on gray-colored background? Remember that our audience analysis included the presentation's *where* as well as its *who*. Will the lighting be conducive to the slides' visibility? Notice that smartboards tend to wash out colors and images, making them difficult to see. Design for the audience and their situation, not for your desktop.

Rule 5: Don't use bullet points

I'll give you a moment to get over the shock.

That's right: you should never use bullet points on presentation slides. There are no federal, state, or local laws mandating their use; I checked, and I'm sure about this.

Here are some reasons why bullet points should not be on your slides. First, just as a matter of style, they are outdated and overused. We've seen them on every slide at every presentation for decades, and we are sick of them. But there are more important reasons too. Using bullet points (or some cutesy version of them) means you have put too much information on the slide. Consider the slide that follows, which is a very close re-creation of a slide created by a prominent author I saw at a national education conference:

> **Student Centeredness**
>
> **Think of why you want to make a change!**
> - Think about your own growth as well as your students'.
> - Start slowly.
> - Study your students daily.
> - Think about what excites them or bores them.
> - Make students your partners as you lead them.
> - Start by adjusting one subject, class, or assignment—just one.
> - Start with a unique class—your best or worst one.
> - Plan carefully. Think of all the details and think of how to pace lessons for you and your students.
> - Rehearse before presenting.
> - Review. Ask your students for feedback.
> - Work with like-minded colleagues.
> - Keep trying.
> - Celebrate success and learn from failure.

Yes, this fails the big-picture test just discussed, but even audience members who are close enough to read the slide would be overwhelmed. What stands out? What would you say is the key point? There is no impact, no lasting impression. This is an overloaded, forgettable visual aid. We are no longer in the days of chart paper presentations, where cramming lots of information on one piece of paper was necessary to save money and trees. Keep this in mind:

One slide, one idea

I see the possible response. "But there is only one idea on that slide—how to be student-centered!" I disagree. There are 14 ideas on that slide, and looking back, some of them had no connection to student centeredness. *Think of why you want to make a change? Think about your own growth?* Those are *self*-centered, not student-centered. But that point aside, one idea for being student-centered is to *study your students daily.* Another idea is to *think about what excites them.* Yet another idea is to *ask students for advice and feedback.* Each of these ideas deserves attention; being just one of 14 items in a bulleted list denies them that attention.

Bullets always mean too much is on a slide. Always. If you are thinking of adding bullets, think instead, "Uh-oh. I must have made a mistake. This slide is overloaded."

Rule 6: Avoid distractors

When Amy Illingworth talked to me about meaningful professional learning experiences and presentations she had experienced, she called out the value of "slides with a large readable text, not too much per slide, [and] graphics or key words that highlight a theme." Unfortunately, that is *not* the norm.

Like most people, I have used PowerPoint to create slides and have explored that program's many design options. I have used WordArt letters, added shadows, changed the background to look like wood paneling, added images from the stock images tab—all of it! I'm talking about something like this:

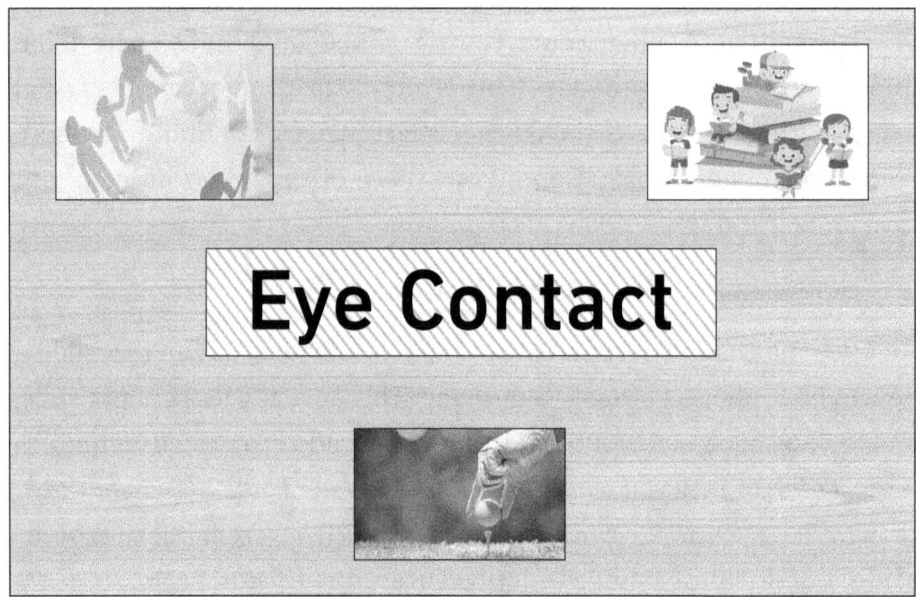

Yes, I got sucked in and wasted lots of time doing these kinds of things. We look at the design options and start asking questions such as "Isn't this a cute picture?" "Aren't these colors so spring-like?" and "Wouldn't it be fun to have different fruits as bullet points?"

Let's get back to the main question: *what do you want your slide to do?* My goal was not to entertain; it was to leave a memorable impression of a key element of effective speech delivery. Everything I added took attention away from my point. How does a "wood paneled" background contribute to remembering eye contact? How do 3-D people with no eyes reinforce eye contact?

Just because it can be done doesn't mean it should be done. There are many slide creation programs out there—Canva and Pitch, to name just two—and they offer all kinds of templates that are garbaged up before you do anything. The templates demonstrate what *not* to do. Worse, if you aren't satisfied with the template, there are options allowing you to decorate it even more (and by that, of course, I mean they allow you to distract audience members even further). I'm fighting an uphill battle here, but your audience will appreciate it if you join me in the battle. Always strive for simplicity. Here is the slide I use now:

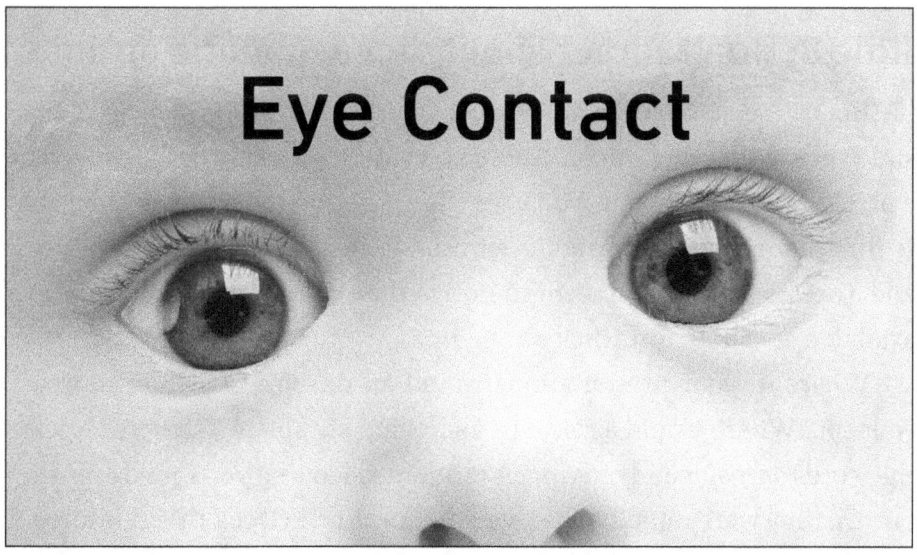

Rule 7: Use meaningful images

Notice that my eye contact slide shows an image that suggests eye contact. There needs to be congruence between the concept and what you show on the slide. And feel free to make the image fill the screen.

A little picture box up in the corner is how everyone does it, but that is because no one taught us that there is another, better way. If a picture is worth a thousand words, choose a good picture and make it large.

Images are useful for other reasons, too. Recall Keith Young's visit to a middle school with his nephew. In addition to the problems he talked about (see Chapter 2), Keith noted that the principal had a slide deck of "People to Know" at the school. One slide showed the name of the school's attendance officer; the next, the name of the 8th grade dean; and so on. What was missing? Yes, these slides were missing contact information, but more important, they were missing photos of the people named. Adding images would have been so easy. It would have given students a sense of the people in the school and some comfort on Day One from seeing familiar faces even if they had forgotten the names and job titles. Instead of a cohesive message of "Welcome to Middle School! These are the important people to look for, and you'll see them in person soon," what the audience got was a list of meaningless-to-them names that were quickly forgotten.

Rule 8: Don't forget about video or audio options

Replacing words with images is a positive move. So is breaking up a slide show with other media. Audio and video can easily be embedded in a presentation. Everyone who uses slide creation tools seems to be able to find the Insert option and use it used to insert a New Slide, Pictures, and Text Boxes, but few seem to notice that Video and Audio icons are available as "adds" too. Click on them.

Where in your presentations would an on-point video reinforce a concept? Where would a relevant audio clip stimulate listeners? Notice the words *on-point* and *relevant*. A random video that you found amusing but that answers none of the five key questions (Does this reinforce a concept? Leave a memorable impression? Hype up the audience? Introduce a topic? Clarify an idea?) is *not* what you're after.

As I present my ideas about how to teach students to be effective communicators, I show video proof that the ideas work. When I click on Slide 47, a video plays of students who have been given no instruction about how to deliver a book report. The students are floundering, and the speaking is unimpressive. When I show Slide 48, a video plays of students delivering book reports after having received specific lessons. The difference is dramatic, reinforcing my point that directly teaching the skills of oral communication has an impact. As a side benefit, it adds a little variety to the presentation and lets me rest my voice for a little bit.

Putting the rules in play

Now let's look at how to follow the rules to fix an existing slide that doesn't follow the rules.

We'll start with a slide I made that shares the six skills needed to deliver a talk well. PVLEGS is the acronym I created to help students remember what good speakers do as they talk. All of what you see here is good information that I stand by and want my audience to understand and remember. Note: You can't tell on the page, but the 3-D star rotates as the slide appears! PowerPoint allowed me to easily add that little feature with just a click!

Six Skills of Effective Performance

PVLEGS

- **Poise**—Make sure you look calm and confident and avoid fidgeting, shuffling, nervous tics
- **Voice**—Make sure every word is heard
- **Life**—Add emotion, passion, feeling to your spoken words
- **Eye contact**—Look at each member of the audience
- **Gestures**—Use hand, face, and body postures that contribute to your words
- **Speed**—Vary your speed, speeding up, slowing down, and pausing to add emphasis

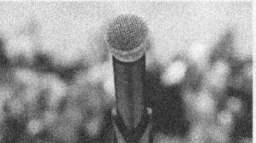

Complete sentences? A mistake. I don't want my audience reading along, so I altered it to include key words only.

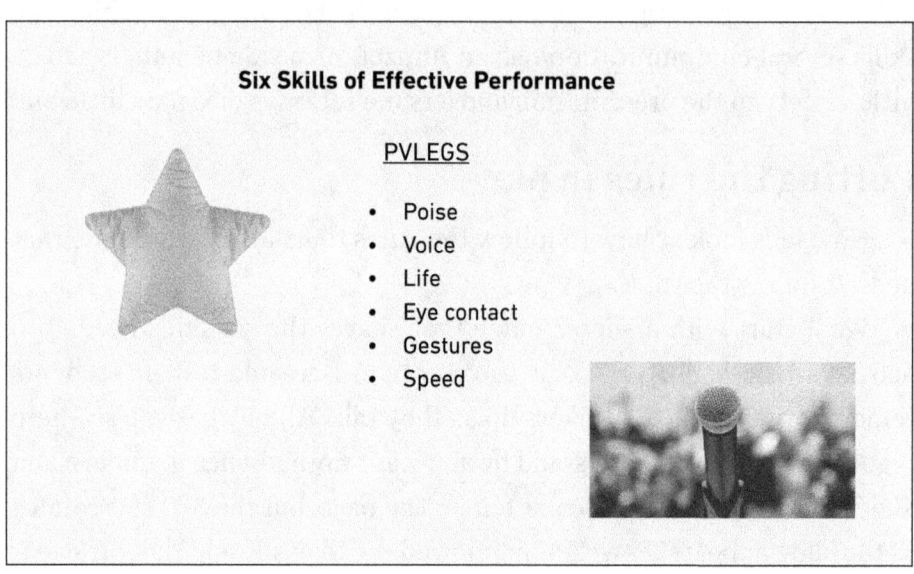

The 3-D star? That's right—pointless (the presentation has nothing to do with stars) and distracting (the audience is watching the star rotate and not paying full attention to the ideas I am trying to present).

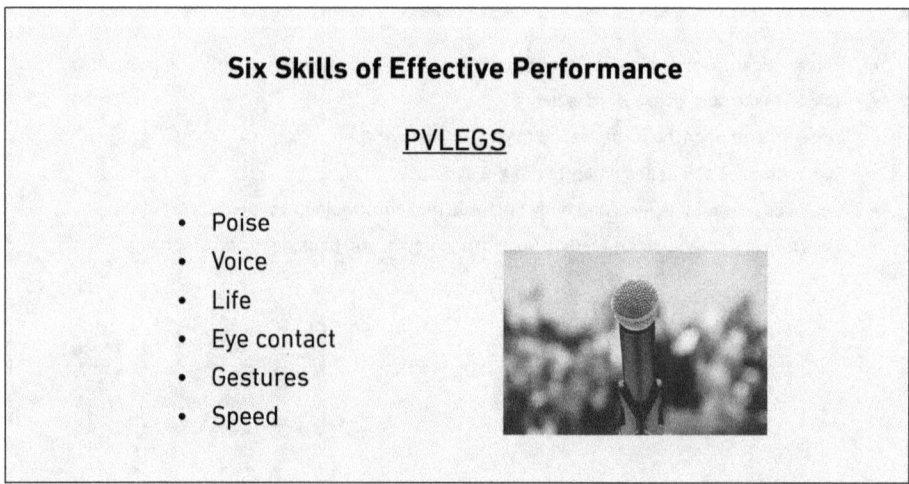

But how will this look at the back of the room? You are having a difficult time reading that little font on this page, and I believe that many in my audience will have a difficult time also.

Six Skills of Effective Performance

PVLEGS

- Poise
- Voice
- Life
- Eye contact
- Gestures
- Speed

Bullet points? Never!

Six Skills of Effective Performance

PVLEGS

Poise
Voice
Life
Eye contact
Gestures
Speed

The image? Yes, it is related to one kind of speaking (in front of a large audience), but the six skills apply to all types of speaking. I want students to use these skills in class discussions, when sharing answers with the class, when speaking to an individual . . . every time they speak. What picture represents each skill instead of one type of speaking? And why put all six skills on one slide? Don't they all deserve attention?

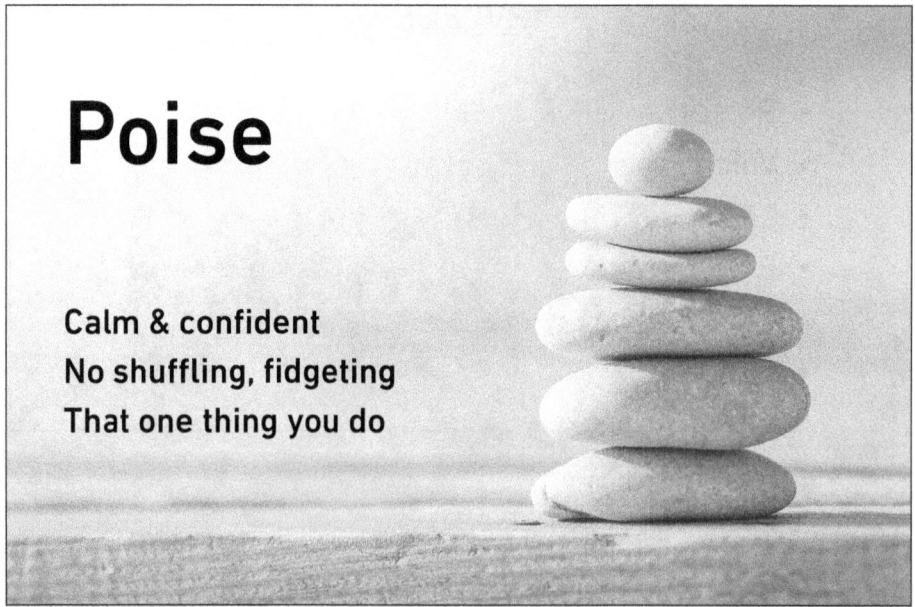

Still too many words. I am speaking to the audience, and it is my job to explain each of the skills. Do the words on the slide reinforce my speaking or distract? I show this slide with the words. I believe they reinforce my spoken words, but I wouldn't argue with you if you thought they could be left off the slide. You can see the rest of the slides in color at BeforeYouSayAWord.net, but you get a sense of the process that you need to go through to clean up slides you have created for past presentations.

Habits die hard. In my work with school leaders, many are not ready to move all the way from the opening slide in my example to the last slide. That's fine. Start the process. Stop where it is comfortable for you.

You will still be well ahead of most. I'm confident that at some point in the future, you'll start presentation design with new thinking and save massive amounts of time previously spent adding fluff and distractors that hurt your talk.

I'll let Theresa Stager have the last words here. Perhaps they will provide some additional motivation for you.

> One of the best presentations I have ever seen was a keynote at a technology conference. It was a young female presenter, and her keynote was full of stories—one about her family, her upbringing, her struggles in her career, her current job, and so on. About 80 percent of the slides she used had zero words on them. They were photos that connected to that section of her message. I wasn't sure at the time if my takeaways would be as strong as they would have been with text and bullets on the slides, but I remember it probably 15 years later as one of my favorite keynotes.

Advice on Presenting Yourself

Although this chapter's title is about presenting your message, I want to add a bit about presenting yourself. You are aware that teachers go home after the school day and change clothes before they come back for Back-to-School Night. They aren't trying to fool anyone or be someone they aren't; they are adapting to the situation. They did audience analysis. Instead of sitting on the "reading rug" with 3rd graders at story time or helping the tech crew make sets for the fall one-act play presentations, they are in front of the room addressing adults, and the adults expect to see a professional appearance. The teachers do what all speakers should do: present themselves in a way that is consistent with the purpose of the presentation's topic and the type of audience they are addressing.

Most of us have a personal style we are comfortable with. That's fine, but I encourage you to consider expanding your style. My wife gave me some wonderful advice when I started consulting. Denver, where we live, is quite casual. For most of my talks, I wore slacks and an untucked, Hawaiian print shirt. Casual, and, I thought, *distinctive* for an education consultant. It seemed to work in Colorado and California, where most of my work took me. Then I got a call to do a presentation in New York City. Anne suggested a suit and tie, thinking the East Coast was more formal. I thought Tommy Bahama *was* formal. The shirts were the most expensive things I, a teacher, owned! But I relented and bought a suit. And I'm so glad I did. Every man in the audience of education leaders was wearing a suit and tie. I would have looked (and felt) out of place in my default style.

I understand "be true to yourself," but I also understand reality. Dressing more or less as your research has indicated your audience will be dressed is another connector of sorts—another way to bridge the gap between speaker and listeners. I appreciated the superintendent who came to do classroom visits dressed less formally than when he presented to the school board. It indicated that he was thinking about us—and not trying to stand out as being on a different level from us.

I'll talk more about digital presentations shortly, but while we're on the subject of presenting yourself, let me make a comment about presenting yourself virtually. My son was conducting a video job interview. The applicant appeared on screen—or at least the top half of her head did. On Jason's computer, the bottom half of the screen was the applicant's head from the bridge of the nose up. The top half of the screen showed the ceiling of her house. Because the applicant was wearing glasses, he could see the reflection of a *Family Guy* episode she had playing during the interview. You can't read this story without thinking how foolish the applicant was. You can't read this story without also thinking of several instances of virtual fails that you have witnessed over the last couple of years. Part of presenting yourself includes understanding what is on camera with you and creating an impressive image for viewers. Do you think about how you look in the thumbnail? How the room around you looks? What judgments are being made when you are full screen? We absolutely *do* judge books by their covers, and we at least partially judge you by your thumbnail.

Advice for Deciding When Virtual Is Better

During the COVID-19 pandemic, all of us were forced to teach in a virtual environment, which meant we all became virtual presenters. Yes, some people were using videoconferencing tools in the Before Times, but the vast majority of education meetings, workshops, conferences, discussions, coaching, and more were in person. The pandemic made us aware of digital tools we may not have considered before and forced us to use them.

Post-pandemic, we can decide to what extent we want to continue using those tools. What talks should be presented digitally? In Chapter 3, I talked about what oral communication should be replaced by written communications. The question here is what in-person oral communication should be replaced with digital oral communication.

Consider convenience

When you think of the nightmares created when schools shut down and remote learning was the only option for most of us, it is easy to forget that some of the moves we made had benefits that continue to exist post-pandemic. Jessica Holloway points out why digital meetings should continue:

> Having digital meetings reduces travel time and allows more participants to attend. In a large district like the one where I work, meeting in person can be a deterrent because of the travel time to and from the location.

Michael Pinto sees the advantage as well:

> Google Meet has replaced some of our meetings, and this has been beneficial in some cases. We hold many RTI and case conferences via Google Meet, which allows parents who have busy work schedules to step away for a short time to communicate. Because parents don't need to leave their workplaces and travel to the school, their employers seem more lenient about giving them 20 or 30 minutes of time to talk with us. We also have our elementary administrator meetings twice a month

by Google Meet. It's a check-in with an agenda, but administrators at various schools can simply close the laptop when the meeting's done, open their office doors, and be present again. The commute is taken out of the equation.

Gabrielle Price adds:

> All our parent education events, like when we bring in speakers on different parenting topics, are online. I'm talking about the drug and alcohol prevention specialists who come every year, presentations on what parents need to know about mental health and suicide prevention, information on digital citizenship and how to help your student navigate technology—all of them. Attendance varies depending on the topic, but it is better than what it was when these meetings were in person, and a wider variety of parents come. We also can record the events for people to watch later, so the reach is better.

It is not just the parent community that appreciates the convenience of virtual meetings. Michael Pinto uses Google Meet for initial interviews:

> It allows me to get to know the candidate and to sift through some of the minutiae ahead of time—vetting them, if you will. Then I can summarize to a larger group for second rounds of interviews. It ensures that I can use my time wisely.

Consider the need for interaction

Meghan Everette points out that virtual meetings and presentations do have an enormous drawback: they can decrease the sense of community:

> Our coaching community suffered during the pandemic because it was no longer a community. When you meet in person, you can read body language so much better. You can see the energy someone carries into the room. You have side conversations about families, about where you got those shoes, about that new backpack. All those things contribute to the community. Most of my coaching learning and support came through discussions that carried on during breaks, at lunch, and while walking to the car from coaching meetings. Moving coaching interactions to digital-only limits discussion opportunities and a lot of the personal connection that made me love my role and the people I worked with.

Humans need interaction, and much of that can be lost in virtual environments. An article looking at New York City public schools (Zimmer & Zimmerman, 2023) reported that participation in parent-teacher conferences was down 40 percent in 2022 compared with 2018–2019, the most recent complete school year before the pandemic. The article features this quote from a middle school principal: "There's something important about physically coming to the school, seeing where your child sits, seeing their work displayed on the bulletin board, and actually having a heart-to-heart conversation. What we need more than ever is people back in the building and people being a part of the community" (para. 8).

That said, there are ways to offer interaction virtually. Let's say you would like the faculty's input on a problem the school is facing or the PLC's response to some new research that everyone just read. Traditionally, you would call a meeting. Once everyone shows up, you would hear a lot from staff members who speak often; the rest of the attendees might be less active or even stay silent.

Now, with virtual tools at your disposal, there are many different options. Maybe you decide the meeting does not have to be held in person on Tuesday at 3:15. Tools such as Google Meet allow virtual attendance whenever time permits. Online discussion tools like Microsoft Flip and Padlet may have been designed for student discussion, but they allow any kind of audience to engage in asynchronous discussions. Users can join in any time and post comments, audio, and video. They can see all comments and contribute as they wish.

What if you didn't have time to finish the discussion at the in-person meeting? What if some people need a little longer to think of responses? What if some people would like to be able to record a response, listen to it, and improve it instead of speaking spontaneously? Flip, Padlet, Voxer, Loom, and similar tools allow interaction from everyone at their own time and in a manner more comfortable for many. There is no worry about a few dominating the discussion, and all voices are heard.

Consider the impact

How many webinars have you been invited to this year? How often do you get an email encouraging you to sign up for a virtual learning event? Although a marginal part of the professional development world prior to 2020, these events came to dominate during the pandemic. And they are still a thing because the convenience factor of virtual learning is undeniable. As Jessica Holloway notes,

> Several after-school professional development offerings have switched to digital platforms in order to meet the needs of educators.

That's true in Steven Weber's district too:

> Several professional development programs have shifted to virtual learning. Our district has a Virtual Learning Day once a year. One person can take the course, and there is little interaction with staff from other schools. You watch videos and take quizzes at the end of each module. There are some courses that are state-mandated (annual) trainings. These courses are a good fit.

Steven makes the point that virtual learning is not equal to face-to-face learning.

> While Virtual Learning Days support the needs of teachers and staff, I don't know if they have the same impact as in-person training. There are other courses that would be improved by having multiple perspectives, small groups, and lessons learned from teachers across the district. School districts can check the box that PD was provided, but was it quality PD?

Michael Pinto has the same concern:

> Videos were hot but now they have crossed the tipping point, and honestly, it's too much. The beginning of the year is a perfect example. The staff has hours of required training—Bullying, Universal Precautions, and so on. Then, if I send a video to the staff about the opening of school, it's like, "One more video?"

In-person speaking is always more impactful than virtual speaking. Always. That means that convenience needs to be balanced with purpose. A webinar will never be as powerful as the live version of the event.

A speaker on video does not equal a speaker on stage. If you require high impact, you will need to sacrifice convenience.

Consider your audience's preferences

Jessica Holloway talked to me about using social media as a means of communication:

> I primarily use Twitter for social media. I think it is a generational selection. Twitter use was promoted at conferences and events when I started attending national conferences. It gave me the nudge to create an account and share my voice. I have found that teachers older than me primarily use Facebook and those younger than me use Instagram.

Notice that younger educators have moved from words to images and videos. This led a middle school principal to use TikTok videos to improve his school's culture.* Whether just being silly or making a point about how to care for the school's Chromebooks, his videos resonate with students, parents, and staff. In the words of one parent, "His videos help him connect with our students in this digital world. Our kids need to know that their teachers and administrators know what's relevant to them." A 7th grade English teacher, quoted in *The 74,* an online source for education news, explains why the approach succeeds:

> It might seem like a silly thing, and it might seem like no one cares, but the buy-in from the kids is monumental, and it means the world to them. They idolize [our principal] because he takes the time to figure out what's important to them, and it makes them more willing to do what's important to him. (Bay, 2023, paras. 13–14)

Michael Pinto uses Facebook Live:

> I do find that some videos to parents on Facebook Live have been well-received. They were actually very well-received during the pandemic as

---

*There is a danger in putting digital tool suggestions into a print book. Between the time Jessica told me she uses Twitter and the time this book went to press, Twitter had become X. TikTok bans are on the table in many places as I write this. Both social media services may soon go the way of iChat, a tool I mentioned in a previous book. The concept behind the tools is valid, though, and replacements that accomplish the same purpose will appear.

they were personal, and I think that people seeing my face and hearing the tiredness in my voice and in my eyes helped transmit the challenge of the opportunity in front of us.

Necessary during the pandemic, videos to parents remain a part of his school's communication. What meetings do you have that work as well or better digitally? Where can a video reach a larger audience or make an impact where you work?

Advice for Using Digital Tools Effectively

Let's say that you have decided to use some digital tool. Some of them, of course, broadcast your message live, while others record your message for later listening or viewing. In this section, we'll look at ideas for improving both live and recorded talks.

The first thing to know is that no one attending a virtual presentation or watching an online video is paying full attention. You may be thinking that is true of in-person situations too, but attention levels are at least higher in person. When your audience is remote, amusing animal videos and sports highlights are always a computer click away. The dog is asking for attention. Cell phones are available for texting and playing games. Mute and video-off buttons allow attendees to get a snack, fold laundry, and watch television.

Only individuals with dynamic oral communication skills and excellent recording tools should attempt to put in-depth, important information into video form. There is slightly more leeway when using social media tools or meeting tools, so let's start there.

Better use of live broadcast tools

Computer and phone cameras have made sharing video of oral communication easy and routine. TikTok and Facetime Live have been discussed, and Snapchat, Instagram, and similar apps may be useful for you.

What about Zoom, the other elephant in the room? Many of us were forced to use this platform or a competitor's version during the pandemic, and it remains a useful option. But for what situations? Remember that something is always lost when we move from in-person to digital. Your impact is diminished not only because of the small screen and small speaker on the device but also because of the lack of personal connection. You can cure the first problem by becoming a more dynamic speaker. Zoom, however, can only be used if personal connection is not critical. If after listing the pros and cons of in-person versus digital you decide on a Zoom meeting, understand the risks.

Jessica Holloway makes a point that will resonate with many:

> I have done my fair share of Zoom meetings. The hardest part of Zoom meetings is feeling like you are speaking into a void. With people having their cameras off or multitasking, communicating is even more challenging.

That puts pressure on the leader of a Zoom meeting. Can you command attention? Can you sustain attention?

Stephen Weber adds this:

> Zoom is a popular tool. Unfortunately, few leaders know how to use it properly. There is a lot of "sit and get" on Zoom meetings. . . . Just because it is convenient and you don't have to drive across town doesn't make it the best method of communication.

Both Steven and Jessica recommend adding some engagement elements to Zoom meetings. Steven is particularly fond of breakout rooms, which few people seem to know about. These spaces give participants chances to reflect and participate. Jessica also suggests using interactive tools to increase responses from attendees:

> For example, a poll or "waterfall" responses in the chat keep participants engaged in the conversation. Waterfall responses are when everyone types their answers but doesn't hit enter until the host/facilitator counts down. Then all the responses come in at the same time; it looks like a waterfall of responses. Also, having protocols or a procedure for responding is helpful. In so many virtual meetings I have witnessed participants unmuting, and they end up talking over each other. Using the "raising

the hand" feature can help reduce the awkwardness of people speaking at the same time.

There are many resources that offer ideas for better online meetings and webinars. I have used and recommend *The Virtual Presenter's Guide to Using Zoom's Meeting Tools* by Cindy Huggett (2023). Use that for a good start and look for others when you have mastered the ideas there.

Better-recorded video presentations

As I said, it's hard to command attention when you're just pixels on a screen. Gestures may not be visible, small speakers squeeze life and resonance from many people's speaking voice, and sometimes the awkwardness we feel in front of the camera is very obvious. The personal connection doesn't always come through. So how can you deliver messages more effectively when your medium is video?

Amy Illingworth has a suggestion—proper preparation:

> Our district is working on a new vision for the future . . . and planning to roll this out via a short video that explains the visioning process and the big ideas. We are working with a professional videographer to capture one of our in-person principal discussions. We thought we would be sitting around talking while he shot some video. However, he actually had two microphones that we had to share when speaking, and he made us pause after each person spoke. He asked us to do two takes of what we were saying in answer to a question. I watched some of my colleagues struggle with each take, adding in lots of "ums" and "uhs" and forgetting what they had said in the first take.

> I also saw a few people who had taken time to write notes that they referred to before each take. After taking just a few extra moments to prepare, they used fewer filler words, needed less prompting, and made it through their two takes without mistakes, while remembering all of the key points we wanted them to say. While this experience was very specific to a video we are producing to share a clear message, it represents so much more. Many people think that good leaders speak off the cuff,

without any preparation. That's not the case. The good speakers are generally the ones who take time to prepare before they speak, ensuring their message is communicated effectively.

As I said before, impromptu speaking is difficult. Write the script for the video. Rehearse. Flubs are not tolerated as easily in videos because the audience lacks the personal connection that leads them to forgive the in-person speaker. Note that the videographer *assumed* two takes would be necessary. As a pro, he knew the odds of getting it right the first time. Be prepared to make many takes before sharing your video.

Preparation also extends to properly setting the stage. In the film industry, there are lighting directors and set directors. Think of those jobs as you prepare your video talk. Is your face well lit? Is everything that is going to be visible on screen going to create a good impression? What will distract the viewer? Will the backdrop you choose draw attention to you or away from you? Is a fake beach scene going to enhance or detract from the impression you hope to make or the message you want to convey?

Create a set that has minimal distractions and use it as your signature set. The "Principal's Message" should always come from the same set so viewers don't spend a second thinking "Hey, *that's* different." The presentation set, once created, can be used over and over. The goal is neutrality so that what your audience notices is the message, not the scene.

The Simple Takeaway

You have choices. Many mediocre and possibly ineffective talks can be improved by choosing to present in new and better ways. Choosing the right location and right style for a talk is important, and choosing to use the best tool in the best way will enhance every message. From one-to-one to small group to large group, in-person or via digital tool, formal or informal, thinking about the best presentation design will give all of your talks more impact.

Application Exercises

Exercise 1

How would you fix this slide? Follow the step-by-step model I used with the PVLEGS slide (see pp. 85–88).

> **Examining Differentiated Instruction**
>
> - **Teachers can differentiate based on student readiness, interest, or learning profile:**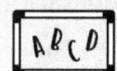
>   - Content—what the student needs to learn or how the student will access the information;
>   - Process—the activities the student engages in to make sense of the content;
>   - Products—final projects that ask the student to demonstrate what they have learned in a unit; and
>   - Learning Environment—the way the classroom looks.

Now, open a PowerPoint presentation that you have created. It could be from a past talk at a conference, for an upcoming presentation to the staff, for sharing ideas with the people you are coaching, or any other situation. Go through the process above and radically alter your slides.

Exercise 2

Review the case study on pages 76–78. Think about the audience's perspective as well as the presenter's.

1. What do you think the main ideas were? How could you make them stand out?
2. Using the same tool (not PowerPoint), what would you have done differently?
3. What do you see as the advantages of this presentation tool? The disadvantages?

Exercise 3

Review the list of talks you created for Exercise 2 in Chapter 1 (see p. 22).

1. Which ones are best in person?
2. Which digital talks should move back to in person?
3. Which in-person talks could be done digitally?
4. Which talks should be presented in a new style to break the mold?
5. How could the "set" be improved for some of the digital talks?
6. Who do you need to share this information with? Your teammates? Your staff developers? Your administration team?

Part II

Delivering the Message

When I ask teachers how the meeting or the professional development session they attended was, what response do you think I get most often?

"Boring."

Certainly, part of that could be due to poorly *created* presentations, but I believe it's most often attributable to poorly delivered presentations.

Ask yourself this question: Of the presentations you have loved, what percentage of that love was based on the presentation content, and what percentage was based on the presenter—how good or dynamic or memorable the presenter was on stage or on camera? Mostly the presenter, right? Even the best slides are not as memorable as a wonderful, skilled speaker. Despite this truth, the importance of delivering a message well is rarely addressed in professional training—not even for education leaders, who spend a good portion of every day communicating.

The requirements for a doctorate in educational leadership and policy studies at the University of Denver's Morgridge College of Education (2018) are typical, I think. There are courses in history (e.g., "Foundations of Ed. History & Philosophy"), leadership (e.g., "Organizational Theory and Behavior," "Leadership in Complex Systems"), and research and data analysis (e.g., "Introduction to Qualitative Research," "Policy Analysis for Educational Systems"). Perhaps the university assumes that candidates got communication skills training elsewhere, earlier in their education. But scanning the course catalog for master's degree classes reveals nothing focused on oral communication, nor is that topic included in courses for undergraduate degrees in teacher preparation.

What about training before college? Well, look at the school you work in or the schools you serve. How many offer specific classes focused on how to speak well? Do any have a speaking curriculum, similar to the math curriculum, reading curriculum, or science curriculum? We make students talk in every class, but we rarely provide direct instruction about *how* to talk well.

Your education didn't help you, then, so can you get help on your own? Books for facilitators, trainers, and administrators offer ideas for team building, questions that can be used to facilitate discussion, design ideas for culturally sensitive instruction, and collaborative activities to use during workshops among other things. Your district's human resources department may give you wording to use when meeting with a teacher and the association representative, and the central office may have a script to help you talk about some sensitive issues. None of those, however, address the key skills needed *while* you speak. So that's what I'll do now.

Part II of this book is considerably shorter than Part I, which is not to suggest that the content is less important; it isn't. In fact, if you only have time to work on ideas presented in one part, choose this one. Improved slides will be noticed and enjoyed, but powerful delivery will be appreciated even more.

This section is shorter because I can only point you in the right direction. Here, on the page, I can't give you an example of a poorly spoken talk—you need to hear it. Likewise, I can't provide an example of exemplary delivery. Yes, I can tell you to listen to Martin Luther King Jr.'s "I Have a Dream" speech and pay attention to how he effectively uses speed variation and brilliantly increases emotion in the last three minutes of his speech, but I can't put that audio into the book. (You can, however, visit this book's website, BeforeYouSayAWord.net, for links, model talks, and more.) Here, I'm only going to tell you what good speakers do and tell you how to practice their techniques. The hard work is up to you.

While you can change a slide design in a few minutes, you can't go from being a tolerable talker to an engaging, memorable, thrilling-to-listen-to speaker quite so quickly or easily. Growth will be incremental. Bit by bit, you will become more engaging.

There is one more point that I want to address—a concern I'd like to lay to rest. *Your job as a speaker is to communicate, not to entertain.* You don't need to be an especially energetic or charismatic orator to be successful communicator. That said, I believe all speakers can become more successful communicators, and the information I will share applies in all communication situations, not just for opening the annual August convocation of teachers.

This section will help you understand the elements of impressive delivery, the skills that must be demonstrated as you talk. We'll focus on two questions:

- What are the vocal skills you need for impressive delivery?
- What are the nonverbal aspects of impressive delivery?

Speaking better can earn you respect, increase acceptance of your ideas, and improve retention of the material you present. It will also make listeners enjoy hearing you talk and look forward to what you have to say. Let's get to work.

5

The Vocal Skills You Need for Impressive Delivery

We love listening to good speakers.

I remember being in the audience when Tiffany Anderson, who was superintendent of Topeka Public Schools at the time, gave a conference keynote speech. She shared some of the wonderful things she had accomplished and told amazing stories of lives she had been part of changing. It was a well-built talk, and afterward the audience was buzzing: "She was such an inspiring speaker" and "I could listen to her all day" and "She was so much fun to watch." Those comments were less about Dr. Anderson's amazing work and more about her amazing delivery.

Actually, I used the wrong word there: not Dr. Anderson's amazing *delivery* but rather her amazing *performance*. I use the word *performance* not to suggest that she was playacting or being disingenuous but rather to indicate it was clear that she had put in effort to be more than ordinary as a speaker. If I had asked the commenters to be specific about what Tiffany Anderson did that made her performance powerful, I would have gotten a lot of "I don't know. It was just great." We all instantly recognize good speakers, but we don't exactly know what they do differently than the rest of us. That's what we're going to consider in this chapter.

I'll begin with an important observation. We have all been enthralled by many different types of speakers in our lifetimes. That means that there is no one single right way to go about making presentations, and different styles can be equally effective. Gerry Brooks, whom I mentioned in Chapter 4, is a principal in Kentucky with a huge YouTube following. As you can see if you check out his work online, he is an enormously engaging and hilariously funny speaker, yet he can also deliver a dramatic punch. His audiences are doubled over in laughter one moment and holding back tears the next. How does he do this? What separates great speakers from poor ones and speakers who are just OK?

What Great Speakers Do

It turns out that the most essential skills of speech delivery are not the ones that most people think. For instance, good grammar, humor, and enthusiasm are often suggested when I ask educators what the skills of good speaking are. But none of these are always required. Gerry Brooks has mastered the *real* key skills—the ones used by effective speakers of all types. By learning and practicing these foundational skills, you too can become a more engaging and memorable speaker.

Great speakers control their volume

We'll start with the lowest degree of difficulty: all great speakers can be heard. I know, this seems too obvious to mention. After all, almost every teacher has "Speak loudly" on the rubric they use to assess speaking assignments. The truth is that "speak loudly" is bad advice, as I'll explain in a minute, but I think the goal of that is just to make sure every word is comfortably audible.

Before you speak, check the room's acoustics. If you use a microphone, test how far the microphone should be from your mouth. Sound is more muted in a full room than in an empty one, so don't hesitate to take a moment at the beginning of your remarks to ask the audience if they can hear you. Adjust the microphone level if they cannot. No one should have to strain to hear; no one should feel shouted at.

This brings me to my point about "speaking loudly." I'll wager that at some point in your life, you have found yourself in a restaurant where someone a few tables away was speaking loudly. You probably thought "Wow, that guy is loud. I wish he would keep it down." But he was just following his teacher's advice. What his teacher should have said was "Be heard," which is very different and much better advice.

Good speakers do more than make sure every word is heard. They play with volume. There are soft parts, "normal" parts, and yes, loud parts. Consider this paragraph:

The characters were tiptoeing through the cemetery. They spoke in whispers.

"Let's get out of here."
"I agree. This is creepy."

Suddenly, they saw something pop up from behind a gravestone.

"Look out!"
"Run! It's gaining on us."

A teacher reading this paragraph aloud to the class would make sure every word was heard. A teacher with great skills would read it as if it were in different fonts:

The characters were tiptoeing through the cemetery. They spoke in whispers.

_{*"Let's get out of here."*}
_{*"I agree. This is creepy."*}

Suddenly, they saw something pop up from behind a gravestone.

"Look out!"
"Run! It's gaining on us."

The talks that education leaders give rarely offer such obvious opportunities to play with volume. They are serious, not playful, right? Perhaps, but I'm guessing that you make subconscious volume adjustments all the time. If a staff member comes in and reports that her beloved pet has died, you'll respond with a soft, "Oh, I am so sorry," but if staff member comes in to report good news, you'll loudly say, "That's great!" Higher volume conveys a mood of excitement, and lower volume, a mood of sadness or seriousness. I want you to make conscious choices about volume in all of your talks. Where are there natural places for volume changes?

The harsh reality is that people respect some voices more than others. A soft voice can convey tentativeness, while a voice with more volume generally conveys authority. No, I am not telling you to speak loudly; a voice that commands respect doesn't require high volume, just enough volume to convey confidence and authority. We could argue about whether soft speakers *should* be given the same amount of credibility, but that won't change the current reality. If you are in a leadership role, practice developing a leadership volume.

Great speakers vary their pace

Michael Pinto warns about what he refers to as "robotic messaging":

There is little worse than a message that is so carefully crafted to ensure a specific objective that there is no flow. In these cases, the speaker isn't self-assured or is trying so hard to be precise that they sound robotic. No one scurries to hear a robot talk.

You have experienced this: a presenter so laser-focused on delivering the message exactly as practiced that every word seems labored. I was watching an instructional video put out by a major education publisher. The trainer was reading PowerPoint slides, which is, as you now know, a huge mistake. But the mistake was compounded by the monotonous pacing of the words. At an unvarying 110 words per minute, it took just about 5 minutes, the length of the video, to lull listeners to sleep.

"Speak slowly" may be common on rubrics teachers use to evaluate speaking, but it is bad advice. Talks that are consistently slow are boring and robotic. Consider that the average speaker, in conversations, says about 150 words per minute (WPM); it's no wonder that the 110 WPM rate in that training video struck me as unusual and unusually stultifying

(Tools for Clear Speech, 2023). According to Carmine Gallo (2014), author of *Talk Like TED*, audio books are commonly read at 150 words per minute as well. The most popular TED talks Gallo analyzed were around 190 WPM, but the talks ranged from 130 to over 200.

The takeaway seems to be that faster speaking is better than a normal conversational rate. Perhaps. And you may want to record yourself to get a general sense of your typical pace to begin thinking about how listeners perceive your talks. The issue I have, though, is the implication that speaking at some consistently quicker rate is the best choice. If you average 190 WPM, that may be more listenable than if you were averaging 110, but great speakers don't speak at a steady pace, period. If you want to impress, *vary your pace as you speak*. Varying the pace keeps listeners interested. Think of an exciting story, a crazy event that happened to you. My guess is that you speak faster than normal when you get to the exciting part of the story. Speeding up has a purpose. Think of a sad event in your life. You tell that story a bit more slowly, right? Slowing down has a purpose, too.

Let's practice pace variation. Imagine the school carnival is coming up. You can build excitement by quickening the pace as you talk about all the activities that will be available that evening. Read the following aloud, being sure to read the second sentence more quickly than the first:

We will have something for everyone! We'll have ring toss, bean bag toss, giant bowling in the hall, a musical cake walk, "fishing" for prizes, mini golf in the gym, and a water balloon toss for those brave enough to try it!

If you want to make clear how serious the bullying problem is, slow down as you detail the situations dealt with in the last month. Read the bolded words more slowly than the others.

*Four times in the last month, we had bullying issues. **Four times.** One student was called names by several others at lunch because he wore a shirt with a unicorn on it. **A shirt with a unicorn.** Another student, a student who doesn't look like most students at this school,* *was bumped as she was getting a drink from the drinking fountain.* **This is unacceptable.**

Vary your speed to suit your message. I have examples of using speed well at BeforeYouSayAWord.net.

Great speakers add life to the words

By far the number one problem with most speakers is a lack of life in the words they say. Whether you call it *inflection, expression, intonation, modulation,* or something else, the point is the same: don't be dull.

Teachers commonly tell student speakers to be enthusiastic. That's bad advice. Try saying this phrase with enthusiasm: "Eight hundred million people are starving on our planet." Enthusiasm is an inappropriate emotion for that message, right? A better choice might be shock, disappointment, or sadness; it depends on how you, the speaker, feel about the fact conveyed in this phrase and how you want your audience to feel about it.

My idol as a child was Martin Luther King Jr. I encourage you to go online now and listen to the last five minutes of his "I Have a Dream" speech. Yes, the words are wonderful, but pay attention to the life in his voice as you listen. Notice the emotion in his voice:

> Let freedom ring from Stone Mountain in Georgia.
> Let freedom ring from Lookout Mountain of Tennessee.
> Let freedom ring from every hill and molehill of Mississippi.
> From every mountainside, let freedom ring. (King, 1963, paras. 36–39)

Those words on the page don't have the same impact, do they? If I asked you to read the words aloud, would you deliver those words with the feeling MLK put across? Of course not; he is one of the greatest speakers in American history. But I can assure you this: the closer you can get to add that amount of life, the better you will be as a speaker.

On a vocal monotony scale of 1 to 10, with 10 being MLK, where would you put most school leaders you have heard? Most staff developers? Most conference presenters? I think we are used to hearing speakers who rate 3 or 4. When we hear a Tiffany Anderson or a Gerry Brooks, we are impressed because they rate quite a bit higher. We hear many different feelings in their voices—everything from sadness and lightheartedness to excitement, sarcasm, sincerity, and awe, all in the course of a 45-minute talk. Strive to have that kind of emotional variety when you deliver messages. For practice, read the paragraphs that follow and identify the feelings that you could add to various words and phases:

> *I saw him on the street as I was driving by. I stopped and asked why he wasn't in school that day. He said his shoes had been stolen, and he didn't have another pair. I didn't realize until that day that he was homeless.*

> *Our DECA teams just competed in the statewide competition. The Community Awareness Project team was crowned state champion.*

Your talks may not have such obvious examples of different emotions, but all talks have opportunities for more life than we typically hear. There are places where emphasis will be needed and impactful, places where empathy needs to be evident, places where lifting the mood will be important. No, explaining the reading assessment tool is not inherently thrilling, but a good speaker, by adding a bit of passion at appropriate points of the explanation, can make listeners feel that the work is important and that students will benefit from it: .

Notice how even messages without obvious emotional weight can be given life through selective vocal emphasis:

> *All students will become more media literate.*
> ***All** students will become more media literate.* [*All* students]
> *All students will become more **media** literate.* [Not just book literate.]

> *We haven't scratched the surface of all that AI can do in education.*
> *We haven't scratched **the surface** of all that AI can do in education.* [There's *way* more!]

> *I don't know anyone who specifically teaches the individual skills of oral communication.*
> *I don't know **anyone** who specifically teaches the individual skills of oral communication.* [No one does.]

*I don't know anyone who **specifically** teaches the **individual** skills of oral communication.* [We don't have lessons targeted toward individual skills.]

*I don't know anyone who specifically teaches the individual skills of **oral** communication.* [We teach skills of written communication but not oral communication.]

Notice, too, how placing emphasis on different words leaves listeners with different impressions of the same phrase. What do you want to stand out? Very few speakers have mastered the skill of adding vocal variety to their talks. Strive to join that elite group.

"But I'm not that kind of person." I hear this a fair amount when I do speech-focused workshops with school leaders. And my reply is you wouldn't accept "I'm not that kind of person" as an excuse if you asked a teacher to work on classroom discipline. You would ask them to become "that kind of person."

No, not all of us are naturally demonstrative, lively speakers. People are wired differently. But have you read *Quiet* by Susan Cain? You should. If Cain is correct, at least one-third of us are introverts. She is, and I know I am. And yet I now speak for a living. How is that possible? It's possible because *lacking a propensity* for something is not the same as *lacking the ability* to do that thing. I am not trying to convince you to be someone you aren't but rather to do the work necessary to be a better you. You may not think of yourself as a great, expressive speaker, but I assure you that you can develop into one. At first, it may seem like a stretch. Bit by bit, you will become comfortable adding life to emphasize key points, create enthusiasm, express disappointment, offer empathy, and so much more. If you want maximum impact as a leader and a speaker, this is the most important skill to develop and perhaps the hardest. It will be worth your effort.

Great speakers monitor their tone of voice

We all know what *reading between the lines* means—picking up on clues in a written text and coming to understand what else the author is communicating beyond the words' literal meaning. We pick up important information by *listening between the lines,* too. The way words are spoken can reveal that there is more going on than the words alone suggest.

Have you been in a situation similar to this one?

Me: I know I said I would go to dinner tomorrow night with you and your friends, but I think I'll cancel, OK?
Anne: We've had this planned for weeks.
Me: I know. But I think your friends will understand.
Anne: Fine, then. Don't go.
Me: You sure? It doesn't sound like it's fine with you.
Anne: No, it's fine. It's fine. Don't go. Stay home.
Me: OK, I'll go.

The actual words: "Fine, then. Don't go." And "No, it's fine. It's fine. Don't go. Stay home." Those words clearly state that I have my wife's permission to stay home, right? But of course, the way those words were said made it clear that it wasn't even close to "fine." Tone of voice is often more important in communicating the real message than the words you choose.

Even subtle changes in tone are significant, and you may not be aware of how you sound to others. In Chapter 4, I discussed how the words you say may give unintended messages. Your tone of voice can lead to the same problem. Early in my education career, my principal pulled me aside and told me that many teachers on the staff were put off my comments in meetings. I thought I had been saying, "I disagree. I don't think that is a good idea." But the way I said this—apparent to others but not to me—conveyed, "I, who obviously knows so much more than you, disagree. I don't think that is a good idea, and you are foolish for saying it." I thought I was forcefully *putting out ideas,* but I was actually *putting off others* by sounding aggressive. I made a constant effort for quite a while to monitor what was a deeply ingrained behavior. I blame years of competitive debate where sounding superior was rewarded, and I don't believe

I am truly obnoxious at heart. No matter, though, because there is no arguing with this kind of input.

"No, you are wrong. I don't sound that way" is a likely first reaction when our tone is criticized, but the audience is always right in this situation. If they say they hear something in your tone of voice, believe them. Are you slipping into condescension? Can they hear frustration or impatience? Or can they hear that you feel you are an imposter? Are you new to a leadership role and perhaps still unsure that you belong?

Keith Young talks about a newly appointed elementary school principal who was planning to ask very experienced kindergarten teachers to stop doing Calendar Math, an activity they loved doing but that had no educational value. He was nervous. His prior administrative experience was at the middle school level. So he researched the kindergarten math standards, reviewed the research (which made clear that Calendar Math did not teach math), scripted his point, and imagined the counterarguments. As Keith reports, although the teachers did argue with him and he did have to use his counterarguments, they eventually agreed to give up the favored activity. That leadership tone of voice I was talking about earlier is a reflection of confidence, and confidence can be built through proper preparation.

Great speakers have "digital voice mode"

What percentage of the presentations you give or consume take place in virtual spaces? Probably more than you could have imagined before 2020. We have talked about common and simple oral communication tools such as Voxer, Google Meet, Slack, and Zoom. There are other, more robust tools out there to help you record podcasts and video presentations. All of them showcase speaking, and all demonstrate just how hard it is to command attention when you and your audience are in different physical spaces.

When you use digital tools to record a message, it's almost certain that message will be delivered through small speakers—those found on our laptops and in our budget headphones. As mentioned before, these speakers diminish the power that an in-person voice has, which means that you, as the virtual presenter, face one more built-in partial attention problem (in addition to the temptations we've already mentioned, like the dog or the laundry or online shopping).

The solution is to develop a digital voice.

First, successful virtual presenters inflect their voices with a little bit of extra life. A person listening in the same room would likely think they are being overly animated, but a listener online would think they are appropriately animated. Here are my guidelines:

- If your face will be visible to your virtual audience, strive for one-and-a-half times your normal liveliness.
- If your face will not be visible, strive for double your normal liveliness level amount.

Test this out. Record yourself. Be honest as you listen. You sounded a bit flatter, didn't you?

Second, successful virtual presenters are more precise with enunciation. Somehow, small speakers produce a muddled sound. On a recent flight I took, the flight attendant said, "Thankyu furjoiny us on taze flight." At least that's how it sounded when it came out of the cabin's fuzzy speakers. Articulate carefully.

A good virtual presenter is exhausted after an hour online or in the studio. It really does take that much extra effort.

Case Study

Ernest was the emcee for the Teacher of the Year banquet. Each of the district's 31 elementary schools, 10 middle schools, and 6 high schools sends an elected honoree to the event. Parents, spouses, family members, and others attend to celebrate the

> 47 total honorees. After welcoming everyone, Ernest announced each recipient:
>
> From Arrowhead Elementary, we recognize Erika Rodriguez. A **col**league says, "Erika is a joy to work with. She is always upbeat and helpful." A **stu**dent says, "Ms. Rodriguez makes me think I can do anything. I love math now." A **par**ent says, "My son loves going to school, and that is because of Erika."
>
> From Belleview Elementary, we recognize Matt Goto. A **col**league says, "Matt gets every student enthused about PE." A **stu**dent says, "Mr. Goto has fun games to play, and I'm not good at sports, but I have fun." A **par**ent says, 'Mr. Goto was a big help setting up the gym for our school carnival. We couldn't have done it without him."
>
> [44 schools later . . .]
>
> And last but not least, from Valdez High School, we recognize . . . .

What Great Speakers Avoid

It is not just what great speakers *do* that makes them impressive, it is also what they *don't* do. I touched on some of these "don't do's" earlier in the book (e.g., reading at the audience, using "public speaking" language), and I'll address them more directly now. Remember that no matter how well a talk is planned, it can be undone by little things. Just as it can be difficult to develop the delivery skills we just talked about, it can be difficult to break the habits I'll discuss here.

Great speakers avoid filler words and unconscious repetition

Amy Illingworth talks about a presentation she and her boss "sat through and never want to experience again!"

> An education leader was presenting a general update on a district program to the Board of Education. The presenter, reading directly off each

very detailed and narrowly specific slide, used "um" and "uh" multiple times per sentence. The presentation felt awkward and painful for the audience, didn't tell the Board anything they didn't already know, and made the presenter look disorganized and unclear.

The "ums" and "uhs" Amy noticed are *filler words,* so called because they are generally used to fill the gap between having a thought and verbalizing it.

In impromptu speaking, you might have to pause as you consider what to say: "I hadn't thought about it. If we .. hmm .. I'm not sure. If we don't adopt this, will there be problems?" Such use is not an issue. And sometimes, filler words have dramatic effect: "You, umm, might want to look behind you because he can hear what you're saying." But the problem Amy points out is one you probably have noticed too. Habitual interruption of one's sentences with "um" and "uh" is deadly for speakers.

> *I, um, think that, uh, our school, um, should, um, not adopt a new, um, bell schedule because, um, students, um, need more, um, passing time.*

Filler words distract listeners and can absolutely destroy a speaker's credibility.

There is an additional category of distracting utterances. Instead of nonwords (*um, uh, hmm, er*), some people fill space with actual words. Amy shared another example from a school board meeting, this time an anecdote about an employee of hers:

> She was doing a great job, except early on I noticed that she seemed to be saying the word *so* a lot. I began to tally, and by the end of her 10- or 12-minute presentation, she had said *so* at least 30 times.

Simon Sinek is a successful author and speaker. His business books have sold millions of copies, and he is a frequent keynote speaker at conferences and corporate events. One of his TED talks has tens of millions of views. I found a YouTube video of him talking about millennials in the workplace (Sinek, 2017). I listened for a bit to see if he had some insights about generational differences and how those differences might affect work situations. But after a couple of minutes, I quit paying attention to his ideas because I started noticing the number of times he ended sentences with "Right?"

> ... and they have no clue, right? So, you have an entire generation growing up with lower self-esteem than previous generations, right?

I counted 20 "rights?" in a 5-minute span of Sinek's talk.

Here's my point: newcomers to presenting and even successful people who speak all the time fall into bad habits. Very rarely do they have any idea that they are using fillers words or repeating a word or phrase. But when they do, people stop paying attention to the message and start counting the distractors, just like Amy and I did.

Like. OK. You know. Know what I mean? So. Right? What can you add to this list? Do you perhaps have a pet word or phrase that you might not notice yourself using when you speak? Record yourself, and if filler words are an issue for you, begin the process of breaking that habit. Put a brightly colored sticky note on your presentation notes or on the podium ("Right?") as a reminder. Keep recording yourself and keep listening for your filler words. Ask a trusted colleague to listen and give you feedback. And avoid defensiveness when you get critical feedback—just like the staff member who worked under Amy Illingsworth did during their debriefing of the board presentation. "She asked me for specific feedback, and I told her about her 30 *so*'s," Amy reported. "And she said, 'Wow! That is such great feedback! I can work on that!'" That's the right attitude. Help the people you lead discover their habits. They would like to be more effective too.

Great speakers avoid odd vocal patterns

Many speakers have a repeating pattern as they talk. On the flight I mentioned earlier, the flight attendant had a musical way of speaking. Her words got higher in pitch as she worked to the middle of phrases, and then dropped off at the end.

> *In the unlikely event of a loss of cabin* **pressure** *[highest note], an oxygen mask will drop from* **above** *[lowest note]. Put your mask on* ***first*** *[highest note], before helping* **others** *[lowest note]. Remember to remove a face mask you may be* **wearing** *[highest note] before putting on the oxygen* **mask** *[lowest note].*

Hers was a musical, sing-song pattern, and every phrase had a take-off and landing, which was oddly appropriate in a way but did carry the real disadvantage of lulling passengers to sleep when we all should have been attending to the important safety information. Other common negative vocal patterns include starting off with adequate volume but losing audibility at the end of sentences; rising pitch at the end of sentences as if the sentences were questions; speaking in spurts ("We must . . . if we want what's best for students . . . work harder to understand . . . the root causes of the behaviors"). Again, the way to know if you do any of these things is to ask the people you speak to regularly or record, record, record—and be brutally honest when assessing what you hear.

Great speakers avoid being pedantic

Stiff. Forced. Unnatural. Good speakers are never described with these adjectives, but they are common when describing many speakers, especially those who are trying to impress.

You can sound pedantic in a few different ways. One way is by reading at the audience. Of course, if you follow Chapter 3's advice for slide creation, you won't be able to read slides to your audience. But there are other ways speakers read at their listeners.

The president of the National Council of Teachers of English spoke to assembled masses before the keynote speaker was introduced. She came to the podium with a well-written essay printed single-spaced on a standard sheet of paper. She proceeded to read every word. She was stiff, emotionless, and unnatural. Yes, varying her vocal tone and adding life to the words on the page would have helped some, but generally, reading a speech is deadly. You would never think of dropping off your child at college for the first time and pulling out a piece of paper and reading the message at him. The impact and personal connection would be lost.

You can also sound pedantic by using overly formal language, as if you pulled out a thesaurus and chose the longest possible words. (Think back to our discussion of *utilize* in Chapter 3.)

And, of course, you can appear pedantic by acting overly formal. Acting high-brow, pompous, or fancy is a mistake. The audience will know that you are acting. In truth, every good speech is a conversation magnified. Audiences, then, need to feel that they are in a conversation. Yes, it is generally a one-way conversation, but somehow the feeling is conversational not performative. The perception is that the speaker is talking *with* us, not *to* us. You can achieve this just by being you. Yes, the best version of you, but still you. Friendly. Relaxed. Engaged. No matter the occasion, genuine works. Personable works. Formal doesn't.

The Simple Takeaway

How you say it is as important as what you say. Don't *deliver* a message—*perform* it. Thinking of all talks as performances will help you as you implement the lessons from good speakers. Be more than ordinary. Whether one-to-one, small group, large group; formal or informal; in-person or digital, put extra effort into saying your words better.

Application Exercises

Exercise 1

Review the following list of speaking occasions for school leaders:

- Staff retirement announcement
- School board presentation
- One-to-one staff evaluation session
- Address at high school graduation
- Senior varsity athlete recognition ceremony
- New curriculum announcement and explanation
- Teacher of the Year recognition ceremony
- High school freshmen/parent orientation night
- Community meet-and-greet appearance
- Disciplinary plan communication with family
- Fundraising appeal to the PTO
- Conducting leadership workshops and professional development sessions

Look at these through the lens of "what good speakers do."

1. Which talks might be high volume talks and which low volume?
2. Which might offer obvious opportunities for adding lots of life?
3. Which might offer opportunities to inflect your voice with happy feelings and which with somber or serious feelings?
4. Where, in these various speeches, might speeding up help you put your message across more effectively?
5. Where, in these various speeches, might slowing down help you put your message across more effectively?

Pick one topic and do a mock "performance" of the talk. Imagine you have a director coaching you along as you do, asking for more feeling, a slower pace, more careful articulation, and so on. Remember, your aim is to be a more effective and understandable you—not to pretend to be someone you are not.

Exercise 2

Look at the case study in this chapter (pp. 117–118). Critique Ernest's hosting job.

1. What are the top three things he failed to do that good speakers do?
2. How would you have spoken differently if you had been the host?
3. Using information from Chapter 4, how might you have chosen to announce the honorees?

Exercise 3

Here's a chance to play a little. Review the anecdote that follows, then practice delivering it aloud, using the strategies good speakers use. Go through it several times. Have fun and try to raise the bar with every repetition.

> *One time, we had a bird in our house. When we opened the door, it flew right in. Everything got crazy! The bird was flying all over, my mom was yelling, my sister was running around crying, my dad was chasing it with a broom. Finally, it flew out. Whew! We could relax. And so could the bird.*

6

The Nonverbal Aspects of Impressive Delivery

Some speakers command attention from the moment they start to speak, while others struggle to connect with the audience. The truth is that audiences pass judgment quickly. This judgment is applied to what the speaker is saying, of course, but it's also applied to the things speakers *do* as they speak. The actions that accompany your words influence the effectiveness of your message.

I'm not telling you anything you don't know. You've heard about nonverbal messages and body language. If prompted, you could come up with examples of odd tics from speakers that drew the embarrassed attention of everyone in the room as well as facial expressions that conveyed enough sincerity to increase the message's power or, conversely, to suggest that the speaker's real opinion did not match the opinion expressed in words. For this chapter, let's move that awareness to the front of our minds. How can nonverbal aspects of your delivery enhance your message? How can you pick up on your audiences' nonverbal feedback while you are speaking and apply it to make your message more effective or *even more* effective? Those are the questions we'll examine.

Advice for Sending Appropriate Nonverbal Messages

The best speakers are often as fun to watch as they are to listen to. If you turned the sound off, you would still be interested in their presentation. I've gotten in the habit of muting my TV's sound when commercials come on. This keeps me from being annoyed by loud jingles, but it also leads me to notice all the things the commercial actors *do* as they speak. They do a lot. A teenager could not have been more bored riding in the back seat of that car, but when she was given a candy bar? Life became wonderful, and she was euphoric! An older fellow was doubled over with lower back pain, but after rubbing some analgesic cream on the spot, he was dancing like a wild man at a wedding! Try tuning in to a muted version of your local newscast. You'll be able to tell from anchors' faces and posture alone when they are about to deliver a sad news story or an upbeat one.

When you pay attention to nonverbal messages, you will get a better sense of just how powerful they are. Yes, newscasters and actors are professionals, and we may not be at their level, but we need to consciously think about what message we're conveying beyond our actual spoken words. Because as readily as you can read actors and newscasters, your listeners can read you too.

Get comfortable

Good speakers, even when animated, seem calm and collected. Notice that I said *seem* calm and collected. Even experienced speakers get butterflies before a performance, whether that performance is giving the nonrenewal talk to a teacher, presenting to the school board, or speaking at a conference. Fewer butterflies than novices, perhaps, but butterflies nonetheless. Your goal is to control those nerves, and the most effective way is to be prepared. Versions of the advice "Don't practice until you get it right; practice until you cannot get it wrong" have been attributed to different people over the years, but the point is valid. Proper preparation leads to confidence. Confidence leads to comfort. Comfort is the difference between an audience that thinks, "You're out of your element!" and one that thinks, "This person deserves my attention."

Be early. Don't rush into a space where you will be speaking. If your nonrenewal talk is scheduled for this afternoon at 3:45, clear your calendar from 3:30 on; if your conference presentation is at 10:00 a.m. in Room 307A of the convention center, visit the room the day before the presentation to get a sense of the space. Then show up at 9:30 on presentation day. Give yourself a chance to relax a little before talking. Take a little walk. Enjoy a beverage. Have a snack. Look outside. All of these are calming actions.

Another way to appear calm before an audience is to find a comfortable position, whether you will be standing up or sitting. Experienced speakers generally stick with a go-to stance that they know works for them. Maybe it's placing one leg slightly in front of the other or standing with their legs shoulder width apart. Maybe it's one hand on the hip or arms crossed or holding the sides of the podium. All can be effective. Pros also have a go-to seated position, which might be legs side by side and feet flat on the floor, legs crossed, hands clasped resting on the desk, hands flat resting on the desk. They leave these "set positions" only when leaving them will accomplish a purpose—to emphasize a point, to go to a demonstration area—but come back to it once the gesture has served its purpose.

Notice your habits. When you stand to speak, how do you look? When you come into a room and sit down, what position do you usually take? Experiment with your normal set positions. What stance will keep you from rocking side to side or moving your feet unnecessarily? What seated posture feels powerful to you? When listeners first see you, they should sense that you are in control of yourself and totally confident.

Make eye contact

When I ask teachers what it takes to be a great speaker, eye contact is always mentioned. This has been true even when I do workshops in countries where direct eye contact can be considered disrespectful.

Why is eye contact important? For one, it creates a connection and can make you seem closer to the audience, building rapport and trust. In contrast, looking away from your audience, refusing to meet their gaze, suggests that you are not at ease or, even worse, that you're not being truthful.

Set up a video camera to record yourself in different speaking situations. Where do you look, and what message does it send? In a workshop, are you facing the screen and reading? Do you seem to be addressing only the front rows? Only people seated in the middle of the room? In a meeting, does every attendee get the same amount of attention, or do you tend to look only at "your favorites" or the veterans or those with whom you may have butted heads? Remembering that all talks are conversations magnified, do you look at audience members frequently, as you would if you were conversing with them?

Study the recording. What you notice will be what your audience notices.

Or make camera contact

In the last few years, I have gotten tired of looking at people's foreheads. For me, it started with Skype but expanded enormously with Zoom. You know the problem: the camera is at the top of the screen, but everyone is looking *at* the screen. You need to look at the screen if something is being presented on it, but when you are speaking, look at the camera. True, you won't get to monitor your facial expressions as you speak, but your virtual audience will not be looking at your forehead.

Virtual environments are less engaging, and your listeners are in that state of permanent partial attention, remember? You can mitigate some of that damage by speaking directly to them. That's why teleprompters exist. The words that newscasters, politicians, and late-night talk show hosts are saying are projected, essentially, on the lens of a camera; this allows these speakers to seem like they are speaking directly to you.

There are several computer teleprompters available to purchase if you feel the need for that kind of help, or if you are a frequent recorder of videos or frequent webinar presenters. For most of us, though, just a gentle reminder will do. Put a sticky note at the top of your screen: *When it's your turn to talk, look up!*

Add appropriate gestures

Good use of gestures is probably the second-most common response I get when I ask teachers what it takes to be a great speaker. When they say this, I've learned that they are generally thinking about hand movements: emphatic hand gestures, illustrative hand movements, and hand movements that seem less purposeful but keep them entertained as a person is speaking—in other words, someone "talking with their hands." The gestures don't necessarily reinforce the words but somehow add to the overall interest in the speaker. I share some video examples of this at BeforeYouSayAWord.net.

If you've never paid attention to this aspect of your delivery, start doing that now. What do you do with *your* hands when you speak? Do you use them purposely and expressively? Do you keep them by your sides, ball them into fists, or keep a tight grip on the podium or a notebook or a pen?

You might begin improving your hand gestures by focusing on having "freer hands." More motion is better than none at all. Let go of what you are holding—the podium, your notes, the clicker that advances slides—and use your hands. Vary your movements: one or two little karate chops to add emphasis is great. More than that gets old; more still will be distracting and undermine your message.

Be aware that hands speak in other ways, also. Shaky hands communicate nervousness. A hand on the shoulder can provide calm in a tough situation. A pat on the back is another way to say, "Good job." Adding more hand motions is a simple way to add interest and impact.

Gestures are more than hand movements, though. A definition I like defines the noun form of *gesture* as "a movement or position of the hand, arm, body, head, or face that is expressive of an idea, opinion, emotion, etc." (Dictionary.com, 2023). Let's look at some other gestures you can use when speaking to emphasize an idea or communicate emotion.

Be aware of your facial expressions

Some people have faces that express everything. Others' faces are more impassive, more unreadable. If a teacher under your supervision is telling you about a difficult time he is having, he may be looking at you for a furrowed brow or some other facial indicator of sympathy. A coach relating a great success is hoping for raised eyebrows and a smile that demonstrates shared pride in the team's accomplishments. If you are sharing school successes at the faculty meeting, I hope your face conveys pride and appreciation. Inscrutable is never really the goal for purposeful communication.

Something as simple as a wink can reverse the meaning of a phrase. "I've never made a mistake like that" with a wink lets me know that you've messed up too. Can you raise one eyebrow? I can, and if you tell me something I don't believe, I might say, "I doubt that" using that eyebrow alone. In a digital setting, where your face may be all that is visible on the viewers' screens, having an expressive face is an even bigger asset than it is in person.

Not all expressions are within our control. For example, a loud, unexpected noise is likely to generate a shocked face even among speakers who have worked very hard to master their use of facial expressions. Similarly, my wife's face turns bright red when she is asked to speak at a faculty meeting, for example. It is clear she would rather not be the focus of attention, and she cannot control the dilated blood vessels that accompany her discomfort. I know many people can relate to that and are bothered by the flushed face they have when speaking. To me, that's in the category of "Oh well, nothing you can do about that." Yes, your audience will notice, but rosy cheeks won't affect your message.

Most expressions are controllable, though, and need to be controlled when they *do* affect your message. Meghan Everette has an amusing story about this:

> We were doing staff walkthroughs with teachers in their own school. A teacher friend was on the team, and we were going into her colleagues' rooms. We went in one and her face said everything she was thinking.

I whispered "Fix your face" to her, which became a joke between us. We would text it to each other in PD sessions. The Bea Arthur meme became a favorite. The point is, having someone to call you on your expressions and be candid about what you project is really helpful.

The Bea Arthur meme refers to still shots of actress Bea Arthur, in character for *The Golden Girls* television show and giving an absolutely withering stare. It might show up accompanied by a caption like, "Whoa—did I make that face out loud?" If you are making faces out loud, be sure they give the message you want to give.

Be aware of your body language

Body language—the way you stand or move or use your hands—counts as gestures as well. When I would walk to a desk and lean toward the student, everyone in class knew I was going to say something serious. "Lydia, I need you to pay attention now" had more of an impact when I made that move. When I said to my principal, "Can I ask you a question?" she replied, "Yes." But her folded arms, tilted-back head, lightning fast eyeroll, and partial turn away from me made it clear that she was not interested in any question I could ask.

Body language, including posture, deserves thought because it can strengthen or undercut your message. You can visualize the body language of someone who has been defeated: slouched shoulders, head lowered. You can visualize a winner's posture, too: head up, chest open. I share the opinion of Kelli Frey and Carol DeBellis (2023), who recommend leaders practice their intentional uses of body language and try to maintain

- Relaxed poses, as opposed to domineering ones.
- Open palms, as opposed to closed fists or pointing.
- Brief, steady eye contact, as opposed to avoiding others' eyes or locking eyes and holding the look for more than a second or two.
- Deliberate movements, as opposed to jerky ones.

When dealing with conflict resolution or sensitive issues, nonverbal communication is especially vital. Theresa Stager puts it this way:

Nonverbal messages are critical in situations where difficult topics are being discussed. In these times, your community will be looking to you for stability. If your body language is such that it portrays stress, being closed off, or anything other than neutral, your community will notice. It is also critical in one-on-one meetings with emotional stakeholders. How you present yourself at the beginning of the meeting and throughout will help or hurt the tone.

Maintaining an open body posture, steady eye contact, and calm facial expressions can help create a safe space for open dialogue, showing respect for the other person's perspective and emotions.

Intentional gestures—hand, face, and body motions—well used will make you a much more effective and engaging communicator.

Notice and work on eliminating tics

I noticed something every time I talked with my coworker David. When he told stories, he had his hands open, hanging down in front of his pockets with palms in. As he talked, he slapped his pockets. It went something like this:

> *It was crazy.* [Moves right hand six inches forward and then back again to slap his right pocket] *I didn't know what to do.* [Moves both hands forward then backward to slap both pockets] *I asked for help* [double slap] *but no one came. What could I do?* [Double slap]

This was David's signature hand gesture, in a sense, but it had slid into tic territory—a repetitive motion habitually and unconsciously done.

Case Study

John, a high school principal, spoke in front of a microphone at an assembly of students and parents. The mic was mounted on an adjustable pole, and there was a ring that could be loosened to raise or lower it to different heights. John never raised or lowered the mic, but he couldn't leave that ring alone:

> *Today we are honoring the fall sports teams. Girls' cross-country finished second in the district* [loosening the ring and holding the upper part of the stand so it doesn't slip lower], *and three of our runners qualified for state. The boys' team did well also* [tightening the ring], *qualifying two runners for the state meet. Let's have a round of applause for the cross-country teams.* [Grabbing the top part of the stand and loosening the ring] *The football team competed well and defeated Creek for the first time in five years* [tightening the ring] *but lost in the first round of the 4A playoffs. Let's give them* [loosening the ring] *a round of applause also. The debate and forensic teams represented our school well* [tightening the ring], *and I'd like the team members to come up with the trophy they won from the Invitational. . . .*

You can probably think of many strange things you have seen speakers do—flicking hair behind their ears repeatedly, fidgeting with a tie, constantly touching their nose, frequent throat clearing, swaying side to side, and more. Just as listeners like me find themselves counting speakers' *ums* and *uhs,* listeners end up focusing on the twirling of the eyeglasses instead of on the message.

David was not aware he had a presentation tic, and you might not be, either. Ask a trusted coworker what they have noticed about you when you speak. Is there something that might distract listeners? Work to eliminate that behavior. The problem may get worse before it gets better. No one breaks a bad habit instantly, and once you are aware of the tic, you will catch yourself. It may break the flow of your talk a little as "Drat! I'm patting my pockets again!" runs through your mind. Play on. Don't call attention to the gesture or apologize for the little hiccup in your flow.

After the talk, congratulate yourself for being aware and taking another step forward in breaking the habit.

Notice and eliminate negative physical messages

Ever work with someone who seemed to go out of their way not to interact with students or other staff? I had a principal like this once. I swear she would cross to the other side of the hall if she saw certain teachers walking toward her and literally turn her head away to avoid looking at them. That was a message well-received by those teachers: *I am not my principal's favorite person.* Intended or not, nonverbal moves speak volumes.

Meghan Everette shared this story:

> Apparently, I have no poker face, but people tend to read into my expressions messages I don't intend. There was a time when the principal and I were in a small meeting with our reading coach. It was about standards and alignment—a favorite topic and interest of mine—and I remember it being a good meeting. Later, the principal told me that I rolled my eyes throughout the meeting, and it was super-offensive. I think about that a lot. I was actually pleased with the meeting and topic, engaged, and had no recollection of why I would have rolled my eyes at all. I think about how I could be reading people wrong as a coach in a meeting (or a presenter), and I also try to take more care with my own expressions.

Negative physical messaging includes more than just facial expressions and body language. Amy Illingworth explained that she once worked with someone who was always on her laptop during meetings. Amy continues:

> That was fine sometimes; however, she was the loudest typist any of us had ever heard, and she would tap away during quiet times of meetings and when we were having dialogues in small groups. The typing became both a distraction and a message that whatever was on her screen (which also happened to be texting and email) was more important than us in the meeting with her. This sent a message loud and clear to everyone around her. People began to avoid sitting near her because her typing

was both a distraction and a sign that she wasn't going to participate fully in anything we were doing.

You can no doubt think of other behaviors that are off-putting. Make sure none of your nonverbal messages fall into that category.

Receiving Nonverbal Messages from Your Audience

While good speakers are adept at putting out positive and effective nonverbal messages, they are also adept at receiving them.

Nonverbal messages are important in every important interaction and essential when coaching or evaluating someone. They can mitigate the chances of miscommunication occurring when feedback is delivered in writing alone, because nonverbal communication carries intention so effectively. People who can see each other's faces when communicating are generally better able to understand each other.

It is all too easy to be so focused on your message that you can forget to look at the faces of those who are receiving it. In Chapter 2, we looked a little at the benefit of scripting. But it is important to remember that a script's purpose is to help prepare you to talk *with* your listeners. Being "script bound" can lead to talking *at* your listeners. Steven Weber makes this point:

> Writing a script is a helpful strategy, but it can be a slippery slope. If you read a script or prepared remarks to a co-worker or someone you supervise, you may not be reading the room. What is the other person saying? What is the other person's body language communicating? Does the other person feel safe and respected in the meeting? Great communicators know when to get rid of the script. A script may help you prepare for a crucial conversation, but when you are in the meeting, you need to ask yourself: Am I more focused on my message or on the person?

Are they engaged? Are they expressing some sentiment? Are they with you? This is audience analysis yet again. Meghan Everette talks here about scanning her audience for reactions when she leads PLC sessions:

Nonverbal cues have always been interesting to me. I think so often we have these PLC meetings in the middle of the day. Teachers want, and need, a minute to decompress, and yet we are taking their hour and jamming it full of learning, thinking, and reflecting. I think about the different postures people would take in those meetings and how I knew exactly what to expect from each. A teacher enters with a stack of papers, teacher edition textbook, and a stack of forms. He huffs as he drops things to the table and his shoulders droop. He looks exhausted and scattered. A second teacher arrives with her notes in hand. She appears relaxed with shoulders down and a serene countenance. She opens her computer to screen share and take notes. A third teacher sits back in her chair with arms folded. Her body seems tight; her mouth is drawn; her jaw is locked.

These aren't the only physical messages you can expect to receive from an audience in an PLC or staff development session, but they are common. You have the teacher who is communicating that he is overwhelmed or exhausted, the teacher who is calm and ready to go, and the teacher who is defensive or seems angry. Meghan commented that in her PLC sessions, teams where most teachers were demonstrating the same posture tended (at least) to be unified in their approach. Teams that demonstrated more variety of postures generally felt chaotic and didn't tend to accomplish much.

Keith Young added this observation:

> As a school principal, I have found that nonverbal messages are a significant part of effective communication and can be particularly critical in numerous situations.
>
> One such situation is when interacting with students, especially younger ones who may not fully express their thoughts and feelings verbally. By observing their body language and facial expressions, I could often discern whether they felt comfortable, anxious, or upset—and respond accordingly. For instance, a student hunched over their desk, avoiding eye contact while I am talking to them, may be signaling feelings of discomfort or distress, indicating a need for conversation or intervention.
>
> Nonverbal communication is also crucial during staff meetings and professional development sessions. I could also read the room by interpreting

my staff's nonverbal cues. If they seemed distracted, disengaged, or defensive—mindsets reflected in crossed arms, lack of eye contact, or closed-off body positions—I would consider it a cue to shift my approach or address possible concerns.

Nonverbal messages are critical to understanding your audience's emotional responses to your communication. Are you picking up all the information available to you? Are you using that formative feedback to enhance your effectiveness as a speaker?

The Simple Takeaway

Actions speak louder than words. That may be an exaggeration, but many communication problems that school leaders encounter can be avoided by paying closer attention to nonverbal messages—both the ones they send and the ones they receive. Work on effective use of eye contact to build rapport and get feedback. Use gestures consciously and well to enhance every talk. Control distracting or negative movements to avoid problems.

Application Exercise

Exercise 1

Recall the case study on pages 131–132 about the high school principal speaking at the assembly.

1. Without looking back, can you remember the teams he talked about? What stands out in your mind instead?
2. Would you mention the behavior to John, or do you think viewers should "just get over it"? Why? Would it matter if he were at the mic at the school board meeting instead of the assembly?
3. Can you think of signature tics of people you work with? Can you recall the tic better than the content of their last talk?

Exercise 2

Have someone capture video of you during three different speaking situations—at a faculty meeting, a PTCO meeting, and when sharing an evaluation, as one example. Play back the recordings with no volume. Analyze your delivery.

1. What nonverbal messages were you sending?
2. Did you make eye contact?
3. What were you doing with your hands and body?
4. What did you do really well?
5. What do you wish you had done differently?

Afterwords

Throughout this book, you have heard from several education leaders who generously shared their experiences with me. I am very lucky to have found them and grateful for their wonderful contributions. The comments you've read so far were responses to specific questions I asked. The last query I gave them was quite open-ended: "What communication advice would you like to give school leaders?" Here are their responses.

Advice from Steven Weber, assistant principal, Rogers Heritage High School, Rogers, Arkansas

Early in my career, I had the opportunity to work for the Arkansas Department of Education. Prior to serving as a K–12 social studies consultant, I had served as an elementary social studies teacher and elementary assistant principal. When I gave presentations to high school teachers, I attempted to impress the audience with my content knowledge and research.

Now I know that professional development should always be designed to meet the needs of the learners. Communication should involve a dialogue, not a monologue. As I reflect on the early part of my career, I was more focused on my message than on the needs of the audience. When we become consumed with our message, the presentation can fall flat. This can happen to teachers and administrators. If I could go back in time, I would spend more time prior to the professional development seeking input on the needs of the staff, the desired outcomes, and the prior experiences of the educators related to the topics addressed. I regret that I did not make the professional development more interactive. The experts were in the room, and I was trying to act like an expert.

Advice from Michael Pinto, principal of James Cole Elementary School, Lafayette, Indiana

I wish I had known to just be myself. Too many people try to outshout or cheerlead their way through a presentation. Just be yourself. I also wish I had known the power of turn and talk. Pose a question and then ask for dialogue at the table. This benefits both the introverts and extroverts in your audience.

Be humble is another good one. When communicating, don't make things up. If you don't know the answer, say so. Also, recognize that there are people in your audience that want to know expectations, so offer them. There are also people in your audience who have value to offer. Mine that whenever possible. People want to be heard. There is great value in conversation and the simple phrases "What's on your mind?" and "What can I do for you?"

I also remember the words I gave to my secretary on September 11, 2001, which I now recognize as good advice for anyone with a leadership role in a school: "You have to be the rock today. You have to be strong. You can come cry in my office and cry when you get home, but today, people need to see calm. They need you to be the rock."

Advice from Keith Young, education writer and trainer and former principal, teacher, and staff developer

Always keep the channels of communication open. In my tenure as an educational leader, I've seen a multitude of situations where potential conflicts could have been defused or even avoided altogether through the simple act of effective communication. Communication is a two-way process that involves not just talking, but also actively listening to your team.

In reflection, the most important talk I ever gave was not a convocation address or keynote speech, but a conversation I had with my staff after a significant policy change. It wasn't the grandeur of the occasion that made it important but the clear, honest, and compassionate communication. This incident taught me that the real impact of a leader lies not in grand gestures but in everyday interactions that build trust, morale, and a shared vision.

- *Listen actively.* Give your complete attention to the speaker and show your interest through nonverbal cues. Active listening builds trust and encourages open communication.
- *Be clear and concise.* Avoid jargon and unnecessary complexity. Your message should be easy to understand, irrespective of the audience. Ditch the acronym if possible.
- *Be empathetic.* Put yourself in others' shoes. Understand their perspective before responding. Empathy creates a supportive environment conducive to honest dialogue.
- *Be open to feedback.* Constructive criticism is an opportunity for growth. Use it, encourage it, and respond to it positively.
- *Practice consistency.* Ensure your words align with your actions. Consistency builds trust and credibility.

Advice from Meghan Everette, educator and a director at the Utah State Board of Education

Someone told me once that leaders change, and the community remains. It is incumbent on leaders to recognize this. Sure, individual teachers and families come in and out of the school, but leaders, initiatives, curriculum . . . all of that rotates. This means that asking the community what they want and how they want it, and checking back in regularly, is necessary. You also have to draw on the capital that exists. Teachers have so many more skills than "just" teaching. Someone in that school excels at making videos, designing layouts, having difficult conversations, etc., and learning what those skills are, acknowledging them, and using them is important to supporting culture.

Communication builds trust (hello, dissertation topic), but it can also break it down. Saying what you will do and following through, repeatedly and in a timely way, are important to building that trust.

Finally, the best thing I did as a coach was to be vulnerable about my own practice. I would tell a teacher I wanted to try a model or lesson, I would show them my plan and ask for input, I'd teach, and I'd be open with my personal reflection on what went well and what needed improvement. It kept me teaching and involved, I was a better coach for understanding what teachers were being asked to do, and I was more trusted because teachers saw me learning and trying with them.

Advice from Gabrielle Price, lead counselor at a grades 6–12 private school

Consider whether you're the best person to speak to a topic. Over the last few years, my school has expanded the amount of time and attention that we give to difficult topics, like suicide prevention and consent education. This work has been supported by our entire school community, but the group that has been most transformative is our students. We have a group of passionate high school students who act as peer educators, developing lessons and discussions around mental health, sexual harassment, and other thorny issues, then delivering them to their peers. Partnering with these student leaders has been light-years more effective than if adults led the same activities.

Last school year, I worked with a few of these peer educators—mostly juniors and seniors in high school—to speak with our 8th grade about consent. Together, we covered how to ask permission before you kiss or touch someone, how to handle rejection gracefully, and the legal definition of sexual assault. Predictably, the 8th graders found this talk awkward, and there was plenty of giggling and whispering. A group of particularly jaded boys was sitting toward the front and a few of them kept making jokes, derailing the discussion and making the girls sitting near them visibly uncomfortable. Some adults tried to shush them, to no avail.

One of our senior peer educators, Aaron, took the microphone and spoke directly to the unruly boys: "You're showing that you don't care about an important topic, and the entire rest of your grade is seeing how you're acting. They're going to remember, and when you're trying to make new friends or asking people on dates in high school, this is going to impact how people respond to you. Knock it off and pay attention."

Instant, respectful silence.

If an adult had spoken the way Aaron did, there probably would have been eye rolls and continued shenanigans. But because he was a student—one of them, even if he's a few years older—they listened to him on a different level. He commanded respect in a way that a teacher or advisor could not because they could identify with him and knew that he shared similar experiences. (What makes this moment really great is that when he was in 8th grade, Aaron was one of those obnoxious kids.)

This same strategy can benefit administrators, especially when they are delivering difficult or unwelcome news. That isn't to say that you need to find a faculty member to communicate the challenging topics for you—your leadership is still important, and faculty need to see you owning your decisions. But watching you in partnership with a fellow teacher can help your staff remember that there are good and valid reasons why you're standing up and asking them to do more.

Advice from Angela Bell Julien, educational consultant, leader, speaker, and author

With communication, especially for a coach, a principal, an assistant principal, a leader in any form, your verbal and nonverbal have to show respect for the verbal and nonverbal of the person to whom you're talking. You need to make sure that you're open, that you're not displaying a closed attitude, that you're not letting, for lack of a better word, the day show on your face. It's easy to let the day show on your face as a principal. I was there for a lot of years, and it's very easy [to slip and let your emotions show], but the fact that that person is in your office at 3:30, 4:00, 4:30 and needs you means the day cannot be on your face, cannot be in your tone, and cannot be in your nonverbal reactions. You still have to be open. You have to look at the person and understand their needs. They sometimes come to you if you're their coach or their principal in a sort of vulnerable position. People come that way differently—some come ready to close you off and some, eager for more. Whichever way they come to you, you have to respond and work through it. It's that double piece. You have to make your own nonverbal and verbal open and willing to work together, and you have to work through your own feelings about how *they* come to you. It's such an important piece of communication. One of the things [I wrote about] is beginning with "nailing the praise," saying something very specific that goes well. If you say that something went very well but you say it in a tone that tells people that something else is coming, then you might as well not say it because they don't hear you. The difference between "Well, at least *this* kid got it" and "I want you to see what the student right here did! Wow!" is monumental. Now you've opened the door instead of conveying "I'm supposed to say something nice, and this is as close as I can get." Respect your audience, and make sure that how you say something doesn't get in front of what you want to say.

Advice from Theresa Stager, principal at Saline High School, Saline, Michigan

Listen always, and when you think you're listening, listen harder. When I was hired for my first job as a principal, the leader before me did not spend time listening to the staff, parents, or students. I know this because throughout the first six months on the job, my office had a revolving door. Not literally but figuratively. It felt as though everyone who came in wanted to complain. What I learned was that they really just wanted to be heard. The vast majority of the conversations I have with parents, students, stakeholders, etc., are with people wanting to be heard and understood. They may come in presenting in different ways—some are very angry, some are crying, some are unsure of what they are looking for. Listen to them. I tell families that I will never be upset about someone coming in upset or emotional because they are advocating for their child. Every student we have is someone's baby. With that comes big emotions. Leave space for processing. Expect unfinished business. Follow up and keep the communication open. Provide them with a way to follow up or check in with you. We are all on the same team. Listen to why they may feel you are not, and then provide the support.

Advice from Jessica Holloway, innovation coach

It is important to consider not just what the message is but how you deliver it, model it, and create the conditions for it to be received. I had the privilege of coordinating a conference session of presentations about communicating as a woman in leadership. ASCD Emerging Leaders

Elyse Hahne, Natalie Odum Pough, Lindsay Prendergast, Apryl Taylor, Chaunte Garrett, and Krista Leh contributed to the ideas I share here.

1. *Feedback is wanted.* Feedback fuels growth. Feedback is best given in a conversation where clarifying questions can be asked and answered. It is super-frustrating to interpret feedback and make assumptions, which often lead to misunderstandings.
2. *Model the message.* Actions are a form of communication. They signal and convey a message of what is important to a leader. Leadership words matter, but actions solidify a belief in those words.
3. *Make connections.* When you are listening to others, look for opportunities for you to connect or connect the person to others. Being a connector as a leader opens doors to the wealth of knowledge and expertise of others for your staff, colleagues, or mentees.
4. *Anchor the message in data.* Others may question your qualifications, but they can't argue with data. Data provides a neutral starting point for a conversation. Data is what it is. And it is a valuable tool for engaging in coaching conversations.
5. *Sawubona. Sawubona* means "I see you" in the Zulu language. Moreover, it conveys that the person is important and valued. Be a leader who believes that each and every person matters. When people feel valued, they are more receptive to communication from leaders.
6. *Be a safe space.* Be a listener in a way that makes the speaker feel safe. Communication requires a certain amount of trust. In order to have trust, the person must feel safe to share his/her thoughts. It is more than an open-door policy; it is an open-minded commitment.
7. *Separate the suckiness.* Remind others to separate themselves from the action. Just because the lesson "sucked" does not mean that you "suck" as a teacher. It is important for a leader to focus on the actions, outcomes, and impact and not on whether the teacher was subjectively good or bad.

Advice from Scott Petri, high school teacher, Granada Hills, California

Don't ignore the listening part of oral communication. Teachers want to be supported by competent leaders they can trust. In every school, every classroom, every day, there are students who connect deeply with their teachers. These connections transcend the boundaries of subject-matter expertise or pedagogical styles. They are formed through care, empathy, and an unwavering belief in the potential of every student. One of your jobs as school leader is to find out how each teacher positively influences the lives of their students, so make sure you communicate with students regularly. Visit classrooms on a daily basis. Ask students questions like these:

- Can you explain how this teacher helps you learn?
- What does this teacher do to motivate you to try harder?
- How do you know this teacher cares about you?

Sometimes you will not get positive answers. But that, too, is valuable feedback that you can give to the teacher to inform their practice.

Another job is to create an environment where teachers feel valued, respected, and inspired, so make sure you listen to them, also. Help them share their experiences and sharpen their insights. Encourage collaboration and problem solving to eliminate instructional weaknesses at your school. By actively listening to your teachers, their ideas, and their concerns, you establish trust and empower them to contribute to the culture of your school.

Final advice from me, Erik Palmer, author, speaker, and former teacher

New eyes.

New ears.

An open mind.

I hope you will complete this book with all three of these outcomes. The field of education has overlooked for too long what I believe is an essential part of its leaders' job: effective spoken communication. You may spend large amounts of time reviewing the literature about assessment, student engagement, teacher burnout, using data to inform instruction, conflict resolution, equity, project-based learning, learner agency, leadership, culture, and a host of other important topics. But all of the expertise you acquire is worthless if you can't communicate it effectively to others.

No matter what your leadership role is—and there are many beyond those with grand titles—oral communication is the most important part of your job. It is what you spend the largest part of your day doing. One-on-one, small group, big group, formal, informal, high-stakes, low-stakes, in-person, on the phone, via WebEx . . . what have I missed? You are in the talking business as much as you are in the education business. Your success is built on the foundation of oral communication.

Now with new eyes, you see how to create better talks and how to help others create better talks. With new ears, you hear how what is normal is not what is best, and you know what to listen for in order to improve. With an open mind, you see how what education leaders have always done is far less than what could be done. You know that you can raise the bar for all of your talks. You realize that focusing on a forgotten aspect of leadership will make you a better messenger, and you realize this will make your life and the lives of those you lead better as well.

I applaud you for all that you do. And I know that you will be more confident, more engaging, more impressive, and more successful by applying the ideas in this book.

Acknowledgments

I got lucky.

In autumn 2022, I attended an ASCD conference to give a talk titled "Blame the Messenger." It was well received. At a gathering for ASCD authors, I was speaking with Pérsida and Bill Himmele, and they asked what my presentation was about. "Improving communication skills for education leaders," I told them. "That would make a great book!" Pérsida said. If not for their enthusiastic response, I might never have written this.

I also feel lucky to have had the support of Bill Varner, a senior acquisitions editor at ASCD, who was instrumental in moving this book forward. He also offered excellent advice about how to improve the book's basic structure and position it for the market.

Fortuitously, the 2023 ASCD Annual Conference was held in Denver, my hometown. At the conference, I ran into Keith Young, Meghan Everette, and Jessica Holloway. I mentioned that I was working on a new book and described the general concept. The three of them agreed that the book was sorely needed. Beyond that, they all agreed to let me bother them repeatedly as I wrote. They interrupted their extremely busy days to provide brilliant comments and insights that made this book so much better.

I was lucky to find Amy Illingworth on social media and Gabrielle Price through a mutual friend. They graciously agreed to contribute, offering stories and ideas that illustrated important concepts and enriched the book.

I met Steven Weber and Scott Petri years ago at a conference, and we have stayed in touch. Both are deeply committed to improving their practice and the practice of educators everywhere. Both were responsive to repeated emails from me asking for help, and both expanded and inspired my thinking.

Katie Martin edited two other books I wrote. Lucky for me, she took on this book as well. As I expected, Katie made brilliant suggestions in the text and offered ways to reword ideas and improve my writing. The book is so much better because of her.

Some of the best luck I have ever had was meeting Anne, my wife. Years ago, she encouraged me to share my ideas. Seven books later, she remains an enthusiastic supporter and willing listener. I refer to her as "my target market." Anne is an educator, too, and I bounce ideas off her to get her valuable feedback. I also appreciate Anne quietly sneaking up behind me as I wrote to ask, "Need anything?"

I am thankful for all of those people and thankful for the good fortune I had in finding them. But I also have to thank you, the reader. It's fortunate for me that you recognized the importance of oral communication and found this book. Congratulations on taking steps to improve your skills as a communicator. All of the varied audiences and individuals you speak with will benefit from your efforts.

References

Bay, J. (2023, May 1). How one middle school principal is using TikTok to build school culture & recruit teachers. *The 74*. https://www.the74million.org/article/how-one-middle-school-principal-is-using-tiktok-to-build-school-culture-recruit-teachers/

Cain, S. (2013). *Quiet: The power of introverts in a world that can't stop talking.* Crown.

Dictionary.com. (2023). Gesture. https://www.dictionary.com/browse/gesture

Frey, K., & DeBellis, C. (2023, June 1). Safe space. *TD Magazine*. https://www.td.org/magazines/td-magazine/safe-space

Gallo, C. (2014). *Talk like TED: The 9 public speaking secrets of the world's top minds.* St. Martin's Press.

Hardison, H. (2022, September 26). 10 buzzwords educators never want to hear again. *Education Week*. https://www.edweek.org/leadership/10-buzzwords-educators-never-want-to-hear-again/2022/09

Hoory, L. (2023) The state of workplace communication in 2024. *Forbes Advisor*. https://www.forbes.com/advisor/business/digital-communication-workplace/

Huggett, C. (2023, September). *The virtual presenter's guide to using Zoom meeting tools.* https://www.cindyhuggett.com/archive/the-virtual-presenters-guide-to-using-zoom-meeting-tools/

King, M. L., Jr. (1963, August 28). I have a dream [Speech]. *American Rhetoric*. https://www.americanrhetoric.com/speeches/mlkihaveadream.htm

Morgridge College of Education. (2018). Educational leadership and policy studies doctoral programs (EdD and PhD). https://morgridge.du.edu/sites/default/files/2021-07/ELPS-Doctoral-Overview-2018.pdf

Palmer, E. (2011). *Well spoken: Teaching speaking to all students.* Routledge.

Sinek, S. (2017). *On millennials in the workplace* [Video]. https://www.youtube.com/watch?v=hER0Qp6QJNU

Toll, C. A. (2023). *The effective facilitator's handbook: Leading teacher workshops, committees, teams, and study groups.* ASCD.

Tools for Clear Speech. (2023). Speaking rate. https://tfcs.baruch.cuny.edu/speaking-rate/

Young, A. K., & Osborne, T. (2023). *Training design, delivery, and diplomacy: An educator's guide.* ASCD.

Zenger, J., & Folkman, J. (2013). The ideal praise-to-criticism ratio. *Harvard Business Review.* https://hbr.org/2013/03/the-ideal-praise-to-criticism

Zimmer, A., & Zimmerman, A. (2023, November 9). Participation in parent conferences has plunged 40%. Is Zoom to blame? *Chalkbeat.* https://www.chalkbeat.org/newyork/2023/11/09/online-parent-teacher-conferences-see-lower-participation/

Index

The letter *f* following a page number denotes a figure.

abbreviations and acronyms, 56
audience
    advice from educators, 138–139
    anticipate resistance and points of confusion, 10–11
    the hidden, 7
    the invited, 6–7
    the judgmental, 124
    the less familiar, 16–18
    respecting the, 7–10
    the virtual, 95–96
audience analysis
    get advance input on perspectives and priorities, 13–14
    how to learn about everyone, 15–16
    implementing, 18–21
    introverts and extroverts, 19, 33
    the less familiar audience, 16–18
    message content, what to avoid, 63–64
    uniqueness, noting, 20–21
    virtual presentations, 95–96

be the rock, 139
be yourself, 139
body language, 128, 130–131, 133–134. *See also* nonverbal messages
bullet points, slides, 80–82, 81*f*

calm for nonverbal messaging, 125–126
camera contact in nonverbal messaging, 127–128
careless speech, avoiding, 60–61
clarity and concision in communication, 140
collaboration, leadership and, 145
communication. *See also* messages
    digital, 61–62
    with graphics, 62
    humility in, 139
    nonverbal, 130–131, 142
communication advice from educators
    audience focus, 138–139
    be a safe space, 144
    be clear and concise, 140
    be consistent, 140
    be empathetic, 140
    be humble, 139
    be open to feedback, 140
    be the rock, 139
    be yourself, 139
    consider whether you're the best person to speak to a topic, 140
    don't let the day show on your face, 142
    on feedback, 144
    follow through/follow up, 140, 143

communication advice from educators (cont'd)
   keep channels open, 139
   listen, 140, 143, 144–146
   make connections, 144, 145
   message, model the, 144
   messages, anchoring in data, 144
   messages, nonverbal, 142
   new eyes, new ears, 145–146
   open mind, 145–146
   partner with students, 141–142
   praise, 143
   professional development design, 138–139
   sawubona (I see you), 144
   separate the suckiness, 144
   show respect, 142–143
   turn and talk, power of, 139
communication channels, open, 139
community involvement, 140
connections, advice from educators, 144, 145
connectors
   content, 34–37
   presentation, 90
consistency in communication, 140
content
   case study, 38–39
   quick conversations, 49–50
   uncomfortable and explosive, managing, 41–49
content, crafting prior to speaking
   connectors, 34–37
   key message, 24–25
   main point, 30–32
   positives, 37–38
   refining the message, 26–30
   response and reflection, allowing time for, 39–41
   scope, deciding on, 25–26
content, organizational structure
   clear transitions, 33
   introduction, 32–33
   repetition of a key idea, 33–34
   well-thought-out ending, 34

content, what to avoid
   careless speech sending unintended messages, 60–61
   case study, 58
   ed-speak, 55–56
   information better shared in other formats, 61–63
   public speaking language, 53–54, 54f
   reprimands and threats, 59–60
   wordiness, 56–58
conversations, quick, 49–50, 140

delivery. *See also* nonverbal messages; presentation; speaking skills
   before beginning, 108
   case study, 117–118
   importance of, 103–105
   robotic messaging, 110
   speaking loudly, 109–110
   speaking slowly, 110
delivery, what to avoid
   being pedantic, 121–122
   filler words, 118–120
   odd vocal patterns, 120–121
   unconscious repetition, 118–120
digital tools, effective use of, 96–98
digital voice mode, 116–117
distractors, visual aids, 82–83
don't let the day show on your face, 142

ed-speak, avoiding, 55–56
empathy in communication, 140
eye contact in nonverbal messaging, 126–127

facial expressions, 129–130, 142
feedback, communication and, 140
filler words, 118–120
follow through, importance of, 140, 143
follow through/follow up, importance of, 140, 143

gestures in nonverbal messaging, 128
graphics, communicating with, 62

humility in communication, 139

Ignite presentations, 70
interactions, importance of everyday, 140
introverts and extroverts, 19, 33
I see you (sawubona), 144

jargon, avoiding, 55–56

leadership advice from educators
    be vulnerable, 141
    build trust, 140–141, 145
    create an environment where teachers feel valued, 145
    encourage collaboration, 145
    everyday interactions, importance of, 140
    involve the community, 140
    partner with students, 141–142
    say what you will do and follow through, 140
learning, virtual vs. in-person, 94–95
listening, advice from educators, 140, 143, 144–146
listening between the lines, 115
live broadcast tools, 96–98

message-enhancing settings and style, 69–72
message planning, 1–5, 12. *See also* audience analysis
messages. *See also* communication; nonverbal messages
    anchoring in data, 144
    key, focusing on, 24–25
    modeling, 144
    unintended, 60–61
    well-crafted, requirements for, 1
messaging, robotic, 110
messenger, blaming the, vii–ix

new eyes, new ears, communicating with, 145–146
nonverbal messages
    case study, 131–132
    power of, 125
    receiving, 134–136

nonverbal messages, advice for sending appropriate
    appear calm, 125–126
    be early, 126
    body language, 130–131
    camera contact, 127–128
    eliminate tics, 131–133
    eye contact, 126–127
    facial expressions, 129–130
    gestures, 128
    get comfortable, 125–126
    negative physical messages, eliminate, 133–134
    prepare, 125–126

open mind, communication and an, 145–146

pacing, 110–112
pedantry, avoiding, 121–122
praise, 143
presentation. *See also* delivery; speaking skills
    connectors in, 90
    digital tools, effective use of, 96–98
    live broadcast tools, 96–98
    personal style and self-presentation, 89–90
    video, preparing for, 98–99
presentation, in person. *See also* visual aids
    being present and accessible, 67–68
    Ignite presentations, 70
    location and logistics, 68–70
    message-enhancing settings and style, 69–72
    the physical setup, 68–69
    PVLEGS for effective, 85–88, 85*f*, 86*f*, 87*f*
    rethink the standard approach to, 70–72
    sensitive and uncomfortable topics, 70–72
    tradition in, 66
presentation, virtual
    audience preferences, considering, 95–96
    convenience in, 91–92

presentation, virtual (cont'd)
   digital voice mode, 116–117
   impact considerations, 94–95
   interaction needs vs., 92–93
   videos in, 95–96
professional development design, 138–139
props, 75
public speaking language, avoiding, 53–54, 54*f*
PVLEGS for effective performance, 85–88, 85*f*, 86*f*, 87*f*

reading between the lines, 114–115
repetition, unconscious, 118–120
reprimands and threats, avoiding, 59–60
respect
   advice from educators, 142–143
   basic, 8–9
   for listeners' expertise, 9–10
   stories, 7–8

safe spaces, 144
sawubona (I see you), 144
scripts, using, 57–58
slides
   bullet points on, 80–82, 81*f*
   case study, 76–78
   complete sentences on, 78–79
   as a crutch, 79
   designing, 79–80, 82–83, 82–83*f*
   distractors, 82–83
   effective use, example, 89
   example of how to fix, 85–88, 85*f*, 86*f*, 87*f*
   meaningful images on, 83–84
   remember your purpose, 76, 83
   traditionally, 75–76
   video/audio options to, 84–85
speaking occasions, amount and variety expected, 4–6
speaking skills. *See also* delivery
   benefits of improved, x–xi
   developing, 104–105, 114, 117, 120, 127
   educational requirements, 103–104
   examples of poor, xi–xii
   overcommunicating, 63
   workplace, ix
speaking skills, great speakers avoid
   filler words, 118–120
   odd vocal patterns, 120–121
   pedantry, 121–122
   unconscious repetition, 118–120
speaking skills, great speakers do
   add life to words, 112–114
   control tone of voice, 114–116
   have digital voice mode, 116–117
   have volume control, 108–110
   use pacing, 110–112
student partnerships, 141–142
suckiness, separate the, 144

teachers, leadership in valuing, 145
threats, avoiding, 59–60
tics, eliminating, 131–133
tone of voice, controlling, 114–116
trust, building for leadership, 140–141, 145
turn and talk, power of, 139

verbal glut, 57–58
video
   option to slides, 84–85
   preparing for, 98–99
   in virtual presentations, 95–96
virtual presentations. *See* presentation, virtual
visual aids. *See also* slides
   consider props, 75
   distracting elements, 74–75, 82–83
   rethink the standard approach to, 73–74
vocal patterns, odd, 120–121
volume control, 108–110
vulnerability, leadership and, 141

wordiness, avoiding, 56–58

About the Author

Erik Palmer is a professional speaker and educational consultant from Denver, Colorado, whose passion for speaking has been part of every one of his multiple careers. Before going into education, he was the national sales leader for a prominent commodity brokerage firm, a floor trader on a Chicago commodity exchange, and a founder of a publicly traded commodity investment firm. He left the business world and became a teacher, spending 21 years in the classroom in the Cherry Creek School District in Englewood, Colorado, primarily as an English teacher but also as a teacher of math, science, and civics.

Palmer is the author of several books, including *Well-Spoken: Teaching Speaking to All Students, Teaching the Core Skills of Listening and Speaking,* and *Own Any Occasion: Mastering the Art of Speaking and Presenting.* He is a program consultant for Houghton Mifflin Harcourt's English Language Arts programs *Into Reading* and *Into Literature.* He presents frequently at conferences, and he has given keynotes and led in-service training in school districts across the United States and around the world. Palmer focuses on showing teachers practical, engaging ways to teach oral communication skills and showing educational leaders how to be more effective communicators.

Palmer's educational background includes Oberlin College, University of Denver Law School, and the University of Colorado. He can be reached through his website, www.erikpalmer.net and the website devoted to this book, www.BeforeYouSayAWord.net.

www.ingramcontent.com/pod-product-compliance
Lightning Source LLC
Chambersburg PA
CBHW060423010526
44118CB00017B/2331